INDIAN CONSTITUTIONAL LAW

POOJA AGARWAL

Contents

Preface

POOJA AGARWAL

A basic understanding of Constitutional Law is a must for every individual. The Constitution of India is the supreme law of the country. It includes the fundamental principles governing the Union and its territories; states and various rights; Executive, legislature and judiciary; Emergency provision; etc

While constitutional law books are not difficult to find on the internet, you should always make sure that they are reliable and authentic. The constitutional law book you buy from a website should be up-to-date with the latest judgments of the Supreme Court of India and other major landmark cases in India. These books play an important role for understanding constitutional topics such as distribution of powers between the judiciary, legislature, and executive. Reading constitutional law books is also one way to keep yourself updated about recent developments in this field of study.

I
INTRODUCTION

A **Constitution** is a set of fundamental principles or established precedents according to which a State or other organization is governed. These rules together make up, i.e. *constitute*, what the entity is. When these principles are written down into a single document or set of legal documents, those documents may be said to embody a *written* constitution; if they are written down in a single comprehensive document, it is said to embody a *codified* constitution. Constitution was written by a committee headed by Dr. Bhimrao Ambedkar.

It took **_2 yrs, 11 months, 18 days_** for compilation. It was adopted on **26**[th] **November, 1949 (celebrated as Law Day)**, and enforced fully on **26**[th] **January, 1950 (celebrated as Republic Day)**.

The Constitution of India is the longest written Constitution of any sovereign country in the world, containing 444 Articles in 22 Parts, 12 Schedules while the United States Constitution is the shortest written Constitution, at 7 Articles. At the time of commencement, the Constitution had 395 Articles in 22 parts and 8 schedules.

- Constitution is said to be the **_supreme law of the land_**.
- The drafting of the document called the Constitution was pursued by an assembly of elected representatives called the **_Drafting Committee_**, which was chaired by **_Dr. B.R. Ambedkar._**
- The above-said Committee prepared the draft of the Constitution. Then, several rounds of discussions took place. More than two thousand amendments were considered.

- Every document presented and every word spoken in the Constituent Assembly has been recorded and preserved under the name of **_Constituent Assembly Debates_**.

ॐ

II

SOURCE OF CONSTITUTION

1. BRITISH CONSTITUTION

Parliamentary government, Rule of Law, legislative procedure, single citizenship, cabinet system, citizenship, prerogative writs, parliamentary privileges and bicameralism.

2. UNITED STATES CONSTITUTION

Fundamental rights, independence of judiciary, judicial review, impeachment of the President, removal of Supreme Court and High Court judges and post of Vice-President.

3. IRISH CONSTITUTION

Directive Principles of States Policy, nomination of members to Rajya Sabha and method of election of President.

4. CANADIAN CONSTITUTION

Federation with strong centre, vesting of residuary power in the centre, appointment of state Governors by the Centre, and advisory jurisdiction of the Supreme Court.

5. AUSTRALIAN CONSTITUTION

Concurrent List, freedom of trade, commerce and intercourse, and joint sitting of the two Houses of Parliament.

6. WEIMAR CONSTITUTION OF GERMANY

Suspension of Fundamental Rights during Emergency. Soviet Constitution (USSR, now Russia) Fundamental duties and the ideal of justice (social, economic and political) in the Preamble.

7. FRENCH CONSTITUTION

Republic and the ideals of liberty, equality and fraternity in the Preamble.

8. SOUTH AFRICAN

Constitution Procedure for amendment of the Constitution and election of members of Rajya Sabha.

9. JAPANESE CONSTITUTION

Procedure established by Law.

While drafting the Constitutional Draft, several provisions were borrowed from various *written* and *unwritten Constitutions* all over the world. *Similarly the Constitution as a whole stands to its effect after having incorporated several unique features and provisions from several other Constitutions.*

III

PREAM

*"**<u>WE, THE PEOPLE OF INDIA</u>**, having solemnly resolved to constitute India into a **<u>SOVEREIGN SOCIALIST SECULAR DEMOCRATIC REPUBLIC</u>** **<u>and to secure to all its citizens:</u>** **<u>JUSTICE</u>**, social, economic and political; **<u>LIBERTY</u>** of thought, expression, belief, faith and worship; **<u>EQUALITY</u>** of status and of opportunity; **<u>and to promote among them all</u>** **<u>FRATERNITY</u>** assuring the dignity of the individual and the unity and integrity of the Nation; **IN OUR CONSTITUENT ASSEMBLY** this <u>twenty-sixth day of November, 1949,</u> do **HEREBY ADOPT, ENACT AND GIVE TO OURSELVES THIS CONSTITUTION."***

MEANING OF PREAMBLE

Preamble means a preliminary or introductory statement, especially attached to a statute or constitution setting forth its purpose. Preamble is an expressionary statement in a document that explains the document's purpose and underlying philosophy. When applied to the opening paragraphs of a statute, it may recite historical facts pertinent to the subject of the statute. The preamble to the Constitution of India is a brief introductory statement that sets out the guiding purpose and principles of the document.

In Re Beru Bari's case, it was held that the preamble is not an integral part of the Indian Constitution & therefore it can neither be regarded as a source of limitations or substantive powers nor it is enforceable in a court of law.

However, Supreme Court of India has, in the *Keshavananda Bharti Case,* overruled earlier decisions and recognized that the preamble may be used to interpret ambiguous areas of the constitution where differing interpretations present themselves.

Forty-second Amendment, 1976: As originally enacted the preamble described the state as a "sovereign democratic republic". In **1976** the *Forty-second Amendment* changed this to read "sovereign **socialist secular** democratic republic." Also, through this amendment, the phrase "unity of the Nation" was changed to "***unity and integrity of the Nation***".

PURPOSE OF PREAMBLE

Preamble basically is a declaration of-

1. The source of the Constitution,
2. The statement of its objectives,
3. The date of its adoption and enactment.

-   Preamble begins with a short statement of its basic values and it contains the philosophy on which our Constitution is built. It is just like an introduction or preface of a book. Preamble actually embodies the spirit of the Constitution.
-   It is a key to the minds of the draftsmen.
-   It is also the soul of the Constitution.

PREAMBLE AND ITS INTERPRETATION

"We, The People of India..."

-   This phrase simply indicates that it's ***we people***, ***the people of India*** who are the source of authority behind the Constitution.
-   This also has an implication that the Constitution has been drawn up and enacted by the people through their representatives, and not just handed down to them by a king or any outside powers.

".having solemnly resolved to constitute India.."

- That is to say that by declaring such a phrase we have actually abide ourselves in it's true spirits to follow and give full effect to the policies and principles laid down in the Constitution.

"sovereign"

- This indicates that India is a sovereign, a nation free from any external control or interference i.e., no external power can dictate the government of India. India is internally and externally sovereign i.e., externally free from the control of any foreign power and internally, it has a free government which is directly elected by the people and makes laws that govern the people.
- Constitution may appear to be sovereign as it is the supreme law of the land. However, a document cannot be a sovereign. The people of India, according to this Constitution have given to themselves this Constitution and therefore, we can say that the political sovereignty lies in *"We, the people.."* and the legal sovereignty lies in the Constitution of India.
- The word "Sovereign" emphasizes that India is no more dependent upon any outside authority.
- It's membership of that Commonwealth of Nations and that of the United Nations Organization do not restrict her sovereignty.

"socialist"

- The word "socialist" was not there in the original draft of the Constitution. This has been incorporated in the Preamble by the *42nd Constitutional Amendment, 1976.*
- This is also reflected in the words *"..economic justice.."* in the preamble. In a democracy, socialism simply refers to a system of government in which the means of productions are wholly or partly controlled by the State.
- It implies social and economic equality. Social equality in this context means the absence of discrimination on the grounds only of caste, colour, creed, sex, religion, or language. Under social equality, everyone has equal status and opportunities. Economic equality in this context means that the government will endeavour to make the distribution of wealth more equal and provide a decent standard of living for all.

This is in effect emphasized a commitment towards the formation of a welfare state. India has adopted a socialistic and mixed economy and the government has framed many laws to achieve the aim.

- In **_D.S. Nakara v. Union of India (UoI)_**, the Supreme Court has observed that the basic framework of socialism is to provide a decent standard of living to the people and specially provide basic social security from cradle to grave. Therefore, it clearly marks the economic equality and equitable distribution of income.

{Art. 39(b) and (c)}
"secular"

- The word "secular" also was not there in the original draft of the Constitution. This has also been incorporated in the Preamble by the **_Constitutional (42nd Amendment) Act, 1976._**
- It simply indicates that the State does not recognize any religion as its own religion and thus, treats all religions equally. It's a status of being neither pro-religion nor anti-religion. It is also not based on total neutrality towards religion. It is based on equal respect for all religions. It embodies the age old concept of 'sarva dharma sambhava'.
- **_Art. 25 to 28_** constitutes the right to freedom of religion
- Citizens have complete freedom to follow any religion, and there is no official religion. The Government treats all religious beliefs and practices with equal respect and honour.
- In a secular State, the State regulates the relationship between man and man and it is actually not concerned with the relation of man with God.

"democratic"

- This is based on the legal status of **_"Damus Cratus"_** which means **_rule of people_** i.e. where the Government gets its authority from the will of the people. The rulers are elected by the people and are responsible to them.
- There is a famous definition of democracy as given by **_Abrahim Lincoln_** that "democracy is by the people, of the people and for the people."

- The first part of the preamble "We, the people of India" and, its last part "give to ourselves this Constitution" clearly indicate the democratic spirit involved even in the Constitution. India is a democracy.

- This simply means that the government of our country is carried on by the people of the State through their representatives and the executive head of the State i.e. the President of India is an elected representative of the People (and not a hereditary monarch as like King of England). In India, President is elected by the people although he is elected indirectly. The people of India elect their governments at all levels (Union, State and local) by a system of universal adult franchise; popularly known as "one man one vote". Every citizen of India, who is 18 years of age and above and not otherwise debarred by law, is entitled to vote. Every citizen enjoys this right without any discrimination on the basis of caste, creed, colour, sex, religion or education.

"republic"

- The Constitution of India is republican in nature as the executive head of India is not any hereditary monarch. This indicates the form of Government in which the Head of State will be an elected person and not a monarch like the King or the Queen in England. Such elected Head will be the Chief Executive Head.
- This concept of being republic is taken from France.
- As opposed to a monarchy, in which the head of state is appointed on hereditary basis for a lifetime or until he abdicates from the throne, a democratic republic is an entity in which the head of state is elected, directly or indirectly, for a fixed tenure, the President of India is elected by an electoral college for a term of five years. The post of the President of India is not hereditary. Every single citizen of India is eligible to become the President of the country. The leaders of the state and local bodies are also elected by the people in similar manner.
- India became a republic on 26th January, 1950.

"*..and to secure to all its citizens..*" - This is a declaratory statement wherein the ultimate objective of the Constitution lies.

"*..justice, social economic and political..*"

Here, these words indicate that the Indian Constitution aims at achieving three-fold justice. It's simply about the attainment of common good and that the people cannot be discriminated on the basis of caste, religion or gender or so and that the government or the State should work for the welfare of the people as a whole irrespective of their social status.

- ***Economic justice*** can be and ought to be ensured by rational policy making and it's proper implementation. Socio-economic justice has been ensured by provision such as Art. 38 and 39.
- ***Political justice*** is ensured by way of the right of adult franchise i.e. exercise of right to vote as soon as a citizen attains the age of 18 years.
- ***Social justice*** actually requires the abolition of all sorts of inequities which result from inequalities of wealth, opportunity, race, caste and religion. ***Art. 14 to Art.18 provides for equality of status and opportunity.***
- The concept of social justice thus enables the legislature to enact and the Courts to uphold such legislations-

  a. to protect the interests of the weaker sections;
  b. to remove economic inequalities;
  c. to provide a decent standard of living to the people of the country.

"..liberty, of thought, expression, belief, faith and worship.."

The Constitution regards liberty of thought, expression, belief, faith and worship to be essential to the development of the individual and the nation, and therefore the Preamble itself promises to ensure the same to it's citizens. In simple words, there are no unreasonable restrictions on the citizens in what they think, how they think, how they wish to express their thoughts and the way they wish to follow up their thoughts in action. ***{Art. 19(1), Art. 25, Art.26 makes provision of such liberty}***

"..fraternity, assuring the dignity of the individual and the unity and integrity of the Nation.."

"Fraternity" means the spirit of brotherhood. Simply put it's that all of us should behave as if we are members of the same family and no one should treat any other person as inferior owing to any factor. India being a ***multilingual and multi-religious State***, the unity and integrity can be preserved only through a spirit of brotherhood that pervades the entire country, among all its citizens, irrespective of their differences. Indian Constitution provides for a single citizenship. All citizens have been given the right to move freely throughout the territory of India and to reside and settle in any part of the territory of India. ***[Art.19(1)(d) and Art.19(1)(e)]***

"..In our Constituent Assembly this twenty-sixth day of November, 1949, do hereby ADOPT, ENACT AND GIVE TO OURSELVES THIS CONSTITUTION."

This is a declaratory statement about the adopting, enacting the Constitution.

Art. 394 and some other Articles such as Art. 5, 6, 7, 8, 9, 60, 324, 366, 379, 380, 388, 391, 392 and 393 came into force on 26th Nov.,1949 (celebrated as *Lawyer's day*)

The remaining provisions of this Constitution came into force later on 26th January,1950 which day is referred to as the day of commencement of this Constitution. (As also celebrated as the *Republic Day*)

PREAMBLE WHETHER A PART OFCONSTITUTION OR NOT??
&
WHETHER AMENDABLE OR NOT??

- *In Re Berubari Case {AIR 1960 SC 845}*

The Supreme Court held that preamble is **not a part of the Constitution** *as it does not create any substantive rights or obligations or powers. It cannot be a source of powers or restrictions on such powers. Further held that preamble is just an important tool for the interpretation of the Constitution.*

- *In Keshavanand Bharti's case {AIR 1973 SC 1461}*

It was held that preamble of the Constitution cannot be compared to the preamble of any other statute. It was also held that the objectives stated in the Preamble reflect the basic structure of the Constitution. Thus, it must be considered a part of the Constitution. It was not a provision as held in the Berubari's case.

- *S.R. Bommai v. UoI {AIR 1994 SC 1918}*

Supreme Court held that the preamble forms a part of the Constitution.

CAN PREAMBLE BE AMENDED??

- As far as the power of the Parliament to amend the Preamble is concerned, it can be concluded that the Preamble is a part of the Constitution and therefore it can be amended by the Parliament under Article 368 but the *'basic features'* in the Preamble cannot be amended.
- Till date, preamble has been amended only ones i.e. by the **Constitution (42nd Amendment) Act, 1976**.

- *By this 42nd Amendment, four words were added in the preamble i.e. "__socialist__", "__secular__", "__andintegrity__"*

ॐ

IV
SALIENT FEATURE OF CONSTITUTION

Introduction

- The Constitution of India has some outstanding features which distinguish it from other Constitutions. The framers of our Constitution studied other Constitutions, selected their valuable features and put them with necessary modifications in our Constitution.
- The framers of the Constitution of India did not aim at a completely new or original Constitution. They just wanted to produce "a good and workable" Constitution. And they succeeded doing this. The fact that the Constitution, for last 59 years, has been working satisfactorily is a testimony to its quality and utility.

1. ***Written and lengthiest Constitution***

- There are two types of Constitutions in the world. Most of the Constitutions are written. The first modern written Constitution was the American Constitution. On the other hand, the British Constitution is unwritten. It consists of customs and conventions which have grown over the years.
- In India, we have a **written Constitution**. The framers of our Constitution tried to put everything in black and white. Indian Constitution can be called the largest written constitution in the world

because of its contents. In its original form, it consisted of 395 Articles and 8 Schedules to which additions have been made through subsequent amendments. At present it contains 395 Articles and 12 Schedules.

2. Preamble

- The Preamble describes the <u>source, nature, ideology, goals and objectives of the Constitution</u>. The Constitution declares India to be a <u>Sovereign, Socialist, Secular, Democratic, Republic.</u> The words, 'Socialist' and 'secular' were added in the Preamble of the Constitution by 42nd amendment which was passed in 1976.
- It underlines the national objective of social justice economic justice and political justice as well as fraternity. It emphasises the dignity of the individual and the unity and integrity of the nation.

3. *Federal government*

- The Constitution provides for a federal form of government. In a federation, there are two governments - at the central level and at the state level. In India, the powers of the government are divided between the central government and state governments.
- **Article 1**of the Constitution of India says: - "India, that is Bharat shall be a Union of States." Though the word 'Federation' is not used, the government is federal. A state is federal when

    a. there are two sets of governments and there is distribution of powers between the two,
    b. there is a written constitution, which is the supreme law of the land and
    c. there is an independent judiciary to interpret the constitution and settle disputes between the centre and the states.

All these features are present in India. There are two sets of government, one at the centre, the other at state level and the distribution of powers between them is quite detailed in our Constitution. The Constitution of India is written and the supreme law of the land.

- Prof: K.C. Whare has rightly remarked that Indian Constitution provides, "a system of government which is quasi-federal, a unitary state with the subsidiary unitary features". The framers of the constitution expressed clearly that there exists the harmony of federalism and the unitarism. Dr. Ambedkar said, "The political system adopted in the Constitution could be both unitary as well as federal according to the requirement of time and circumstances". We can say that India has a "Cooperative federalism" with central guidance and state compliance.

4. *Parliamentary government*

- India has adopted the Parliamentary system as found in Britain. In this system, the executive is responsible to the legislature, and remains in power only as long and it enjoys the confidence of the legislature. Indian Constitution provides for a parliamentary form of government. The majority party in the Lower House (Lok Sabha) forms government. The Council of Ministers is collectively responsible to the Parliament. The Cabinet is the real executive head. In Presidential form of government, the President is the executive head. In India, the President is only the nominal head.

5. *Three Tier Government*

- Indian Constitution provides for a three-tier government.
- Originally, it was two tiers i.e., Centre and the State
- But by 73rd and 74th Amendment Act, 1992 three tier government has been established. (Centre, state & local self-government)
- Panchayat raj system was adopted by way of these two amendments.

6. *Fundamental rights and duties*

- These rights are fundamental because they are basic to the moral and spiritual development of the individual and these rights cannot be easily abridged by the parliament.
- Now the citizen enjoys six fundamental rights, originally there were seven fundamental rights. One of them was taken away from Part III of the Constitution by the Forty-fourth Amendment Act, 1978. As a result, the Right to Property is no longer a fundamental right. Since 1978, it has

become a legal right.

- The idea of fundamental rights has been borrowed from the American Constitution.
- Any citizen of India can seek the help of High Court or Supreme Court of India if any of his fundamental rights is undermined by the government or any institution or any other government.
- Fundamental rights are **justiciable in nature.**(i.e., they are legally enforceable by the court of law). These are not absolute in nature & are subject to some restrictions. Parliament can amend them but not those provisions that form the **"basic structure"** of the Constitution.
- Suspended during National Emergency (Except Art 20 & 21).
- ***The Constitution of India guarantees six fundamental rights to every citizen.*** These are:

i. *Right to Equality.* [Article 14-18]
ii. *Right to Freedom.* [Article 19-22]
iii. *Right against Exploitation.* [Article 23,24]
iv. *Right to Freedom of Religion.* [Article 25-28]
v. *Cultural and Educational Rights.* [Article 29, 30]
vi. *Right to Constitutional Remedies.* [Article 32]

7. Fundamental Duties

- Non-justiciable in nature (i.e., they are not legally enforceable by the court of law)
- Not present in the original Constitution. (Added by 42nd Amendment Act, 1976 on the recommendation by Swarn Singh committee.)
- Reminds people that while enjoying rights they have some duties to do.

8. *Directive principles of state policy*

- These principles are in the nature of directives to the government to implement them for establishing social and economic democracy in the country.
- The Directive Principles of State Policy are enumerated in Part IV of the Constitution. The framers of our Constitution took the idea of having such principles from the Irish Constitution.

- These principles have been stated a; "fundamental in the governance of the country".
- They are instructions or directives from the Constitution to the state and the government. It is the duty of the government to implement them.
- **Non-justiciable in nature**(i.e., they are not legally enforceable by the court of law) but they are nevertheless fundamental in the governance of the country.
- Promotes social and economic democracy
- In general, the Directive Principles aim at building a Welfare State. These principles provide the criteria with which we can judge the performance of the government.

9. *Fundamental Duties*

- A new part IV (A) after the Directive Principles of State Policy was incorporated in the constitution by the 42nd Amendment, 1976 for fundaments duties. Fundamental Duties did not form part of the Constitution. Ten Fundamental Duties were inserted in Part IV by the Constitution 42nd Amendment Act, 1976.
- A new Article - Article 51-A enumerates ten Fundamental Duties. These duties are assigned only to citizens and not to non-citizens. These duties are **not justifiable**(i.e., These cannot be enforced through the courts of law)
- The purpose of incorporating these duties in the Constitution is just to remind the people that while enjoying their right as citizens, should also perform their duties for rights and duties are correlative.

10. *Partly rigid and partly flexible*

- Whether a constitution is rigid or flexible depends on the nature of amendment.
- The Constitution of India is neither wholly rigid nor wholly flexible. It is partly rigid and partly flexible. It is because of the fact that for the purpose of amendment, our Constitution has been divided into three parts:

  a. Certain provisions of the Constitution can be amended by a simple majority in the Parliament.

b. Certain provisions can be amended by a two-third majority of the Parliament and its ratification by at least half of the states.

c. The remaining provisions can be amended by the Parliament by two-third majority.

- These different amendment procedures make our Constitution partly flexible and rigid. In fact, there is a balance between rigidity and flexibility in our Constitution.
- Some amount of flexibility was introduced into our Constitution in order to encourage its growth.
- Pt. Jawaharlal Nehru feared that if a Constitution is too rigid, it will be stagnant and that the growth of the nation would be hampered.

11. *Single citizenship*

- In a federation, normally we have double citizenship. In the United States of America, there is double citizenship. An American is a citizen of America and at the same time he is also a citizen of one of the 50 States of America where he resides. In India, there is only single citizenship. Every Indian, irrespective of his place of birth or residence, is a citizen of India only. He is not a citizen of any Indian state. There is no citizenship of Madhya Pradesh, Delhi, Punjab, U.P. or so.
- Single citizenship is meant to ensure national unity and national integration.

12. *Universal Adult Franchise*

- Article 326 of the Constitution of India provides Universal Adult Franchise. It means that every citizen of India who has completed 18 years of age is eligible to vote in general elections irrespective of his caste, creed, sex, religion or place of birth. This is one of the most revolutionary aspects of Indian democracy.

13. *Language Policy*

- The Constitution has also defined the language policy. India is a country where different languages are spoken in various parts of the country. Hindi and English have been made official languages of the Central

Government. A state can adopt the language spoken by its people in that state also as its official language.

- Although India is a multi-lingual nation, the Constitution provides that Hindi in Devnagri script will be the national language. It shall be the duty of the union to promote and spread Hindi language.
- At present, we have **22 languages** which have been recognised by the Indian Constitution. These are: ***Assamese, Gujarati, Konkani, Marathi, Sanskrit, Telugu, Bengali, Hindi, Maithili, Nepali, Santhali, Urdu, Bodo, Kannada, Malayalam, Oriya, Sindhi, Dogri, Kashmiri, Manipuri, Punjabi, Tamil.***

14. *Independent judiciary*

- The Indian Constitution provides for an independent judiciary as also envisaged as a directive principle laid down under Art. 50 i.e. "Separation of judiciary from executive". The judiciary has been made independent of the Executive as well as the Legislature.
- The judiciary in India is independent and impartial. It is an integrated and a hierarchical judiciary with the Supreme Court at the apex of the hierarchy. The High Courts stand in its middle, and the lower courts are located at its bottom.
- The Judges security of tenure and it is extremely difficult to remove any Judge of the Supreme or of the High Court through impeachment.
- Also, the Supreme Court and the High Courts have the power of Judicial Review. They have the power to declare acts of legislatures and actions of the Executive ultra vires and such acts or actions are found to be in conflict with the provisions of the Constitution.

15. ***A Constitution derived from many sources***

- The framers of our Constitution borrowed many things from the Constitutions of various other countries and included them in our Constitution. That is why some writers call Indian Constitution a 'bag of borrowings'.

16. ***Emergency provisions***

- The framers of our Constitution had realised that there could be certain dangerous situations when government could not be run as in ordinary time. Hence our Constitution contains certain emergency provisions.
- During emergency the fundamental rights of the citizens can be suspended and our government becomes a unitary one.

17. *Federal Government with Unitary Bias*

- India is a federation, although word 'federation' does not find a place in the whole text of the Indian Constitution. The elements of federation are present in the Indian Constitution. It is a written and rigid Constitution.
- There is dual polity and there is Constitutional division of powers between the centre and the states. There is also an independent judiciary. The Supreme Court arbitrates the disputes between the centre and the states.
- All these provisions make India a federation. But in Indian Federation, the centre is strong as compared to the states. The centre has more financial powers and the states largely depend upon it for their economic development. The Governor acts as the agent of the centre.
- The centre can reorganize a state, but a state cannot reorganize the centre. In other words, the centre is indestructible while the states are destructible. During emergencies, the powers of the centre considerably grow and the states become weak.
- K. C. Where has described the Indian government as 'quasi-federal'. India has also been characterised as 'a federal state with unitary spirit.'
- Indian Constitution establishes India as the federal system of government. Federal system means a political system where is there division of powers between centre and State. But Indian federal system is unique in itself as it
- The Constitution of India has some outstanding features which distinguish it from other Constitutions. The framers of our Constitution studied other Constitutions, selected their valuable features and put them with necessary modifications in our Constitution.
- The framers of the Constitution of India did not aim at a completely new or original Constitution. They just wanted to produce "a good and workable" Constitution. And they succeeded doing this. The fact that the Constitution, for last 59 years, has been working satisfactorily is a testimony to its quality and utility.

- So, Indian Political structure can be rightly described as "federal system with strong centre"

V

NATURE OF VARIOUS CONSTITUTIONS IN THE WORLD

Nature of Constitution necessarily depends upon the types of Constitution

1. Written or unwritten Constitution:

Most of the countries over the world have a written Constitution. Best example of an unwritten Constitution is British Constitution (UK)

2. Rigid or Flexible Constitution

- A Constitution is **rigid** if for the amendment or review of its provisions, a special provision is required to be followed. *Example - Constitution of USA*.
- A Constitution is **flexible** if its provisions can be amended or revised by the ordinary legislative process. *Example - Constitution of UK*
- A rigid Constitution possesses the quality of stability. And the drawback of being a rigid Constitution is that such a Constitution cannot be tuned in accordance with the needs of the society as and when required. It places obstacles in the required social changes.
- Flexible Constitution, on the other hand, can be easily amended according to the needs of the society but the drawback is that such a Constitution lacks stability.

3. Federal and Unitary Constitution

Typically, democratic Constitutions are classified into two categories-

1. UNITARY CONSTITUTION
2. FEDERAL CONSTITUTION

- Constitution which provides for a federal system of government is called a Federal Constitution, while a Constitution which provides for a unitary form of government is called a Unitary Constitution.
- In a Unitary Constitution, all the powers of the government are given to the Centre and the local govt. enjoy the powers delegated to them by the Centre.
- The federal Constitution establishes a federal system of government. It establishes a system of double government – Central government, and the State government.

Merits of Unitary Constitution

1. Unitary Constitution establishes a strong Central Government which is found more useful in times of war and emergencies.
2. The Central govt. has all the powers of the govt. and the local or the State govt. just enjoys the powers delegated to them.
3. No conflict of authority and no overlapping of jurisdiction.
4. Unitary Constitution is more flexible.

Demerits of Unitary Constitution

1. Unitary Constitution develops centralized bureaucracy.
2. The laws are often made in ignorance of the local conditions and needs.
3. They are administered by the persons who do not have sufficient knowledge of the local needs.
4. Unitary Constitution is more flexible and therefore it does lack stability.

CHARACTERISTICS OF FEDERALISM

1. **System of double government**: India has two sets of government - the Central or Union government and the State government. The Central government works for the whole country and the State governments look after the States. The areas of activity of both the governments are different.

2. **Distribution of Powers**: The Constitution of India has divided powers between the Central government and the state governments. The Seventh Schedule of the Constitution contains three lists of subjects which show how division of power is made between the two sets of government. Both the governments have their separate powers and responsibilities.

3. **Written and rigid Constitution**: The Constitution of India is written. Every provision of the Constitution is clearly written down and has been discussed in detail. It is regarded as one of the longest constitutions of the world which has 395 Articles 22 Parts and 12 Schedules.

4. **Supremacy of the Constitution**: The Constitution is regarded as the supreme law of the land. No law can be made which will go against the authority of the Constitution. The Constitution is above all and all citizens and organizations within the territory of India must be loyal to the Constitution.

5. **Independent judiciary and Supremacy of judiciary**: The Supreme Court of India is the highest court of justice in India. It has been given the responsibility of interpreting the provisions of the Constitution. It is regarded as the guardian of the Constitution.

6. **Bi-cameral legislation**: In India, the legislature is bi-cameral. The Indian Parliament, i.e., the legislature has two houses - the Lok Sabha and the Rajya Sabha. The Rajya is the upper house of the Parliament representing the States while the Lok Sabha is the lower house representing the people in general.

Merits of Federal Constitution

1. Federal Constitution better protects the Regional and Local interest.
2. Subjects of local interest are entrusted to the regional govt. and that of the national importance are entrusted to the Central govt. Therefore, the local Legislatures gets an opportunity to make laws according to the local needs.
3. A federal Constitution tends to develop decentralization.
4. A federal Constitution is therefore more democratic in nature.

Demerits of Federal Constitution

1. A Federal Constitution leads to the establishment of a weak government. The Central govt. has no direct control over the matters allotted to the

regional governments.

2. Such weaknesses are evident on the times of emergencies.
3. Possibility of development of regionalism.
4. Citizens may show a greater loyalty towards their region rather than the Union. This may be a serious threat to the national unity.
5. A Federal Constitution, a conflict of authority and overlapping of jurisdiction may always arise and in such a govt., there is a possibility of confusion regarding the responsibility for work to be done and duplication of work.
6. Duplication of work may always lead to more administrative expenses.
7. A Federal Constitution is rigid in nature and therefore it cannot be amended according to the needs.
8. Such double system of govt. is also a cause of the delayed execution and implementation of plans and projects.

INDIAN CONSTITUTION WHETHER FEDERAL OR UNITARY??

- No doubt, Indian Constitution is a blend of features of both Federal as well as Unitary Constitution. But, after observing all the features of Indian Constitution, it is conclusive that it is federal with a unitary bias.
- ***Comparative analysis of essential features of federal Constitution and Indian Constitution***

A federal Constitution possesses the following characteristics -

1. ***System of double governments***

In a federal Constitution, there exists a double government i.e., the Central government and the State or the regional Governments. This feature is also found under the Indian Constitution.

2. ***Distribution of powers***

A Federal Constitution essentially provides for distribution of powers between the Central and the State Governments. Both the governments are coordinate and independent in their sphere and not subordinate to one another.

3. Rigid and Written Constitution

It is not necessary that a federal Constitution should always be a written Constitution but it has been observed that in most of the countries having a Federal Constitution are generally written Constitutions. India too has a written Constitution and under Art.368, three modes of amendment have been provided, which renders it neither absolutely rigid nor absolutely flexible.

4. <u>Independent judiciary</u>

Independence of judiciary is necessary to maintain the federal structure intact. Various provisions to ensure the independence of judiciary are-

- Appointment of judges by the Head of the executive or through independent Commission.
- Difficult procedure for their removal(impeachment)
- No variation in conditions of their services to their disadvantage after their appointment.
- Prohibition of any discussion as to the conduct of any judge.
- Security of tenure.

5. **Supremacy of Constitution -**

- In India, Constitution is the supreme of the land.
- All three organs of the Indian democracy i.e., the executive, legislature and the judiciary, all have to abide by and follow the Constitutional principles.
- Here, judiciary is regarded as the guardian of Indian Constitution and therefore the power of judicial review holds a very significant place as far as the power of judiciary as the guardian of Constitution is concerned.
- In USA's Constitution also, since it establishes a federalism, the Constitution is supreme like India.
- In England, there is supremacy of the Parliament. In England, the Parliament is sovereign.
- Supremacy of Constitution is also one of the basic structures in the Indian Constitution which cannot be disturbed in the name of a Constitutional amendment.
- Power of judicial review as provided under Article 13 is a reflection of the independence of the judiciary.

6CASES ON NATURE OF INDIAN CONSTITUTION

- ___State of West Bengal v. UoI {AIR 1963 SC 1241}___- Supreme Court held that Indian Constitution is **not truly federal because the States are not coordinate with the Union.**
- ___Kuldeep Nayyar v. UoI {AIR 2006 SC 3127}___ - Supreme Court held that **federal principle is the basic feature of the Constitution however federation leans in favour of strong Centre.**

OPINIONS REGARDING NATURE OF INDIAN CONSTITUTION

- ___K.C. Whare___has characterized Indian Constitution as ___quasi-federal.___
- ___Jennings___opined that Indian Constitution should be described as ___federation with a strongcentralizing tendency.___
- ___Austin___suggested that Indian Constitution can be called federal, "___a Co-operative federalism.___

VI
STATE

Article 1 (1) of the Indian Constitution provides that- "***India, that is Bharat, shall be a Union ofStates.***" Thus, Article 1 describes the name by which our Country shall be called or known. The expression "Union of States" has been taken from the Preamble to the North America (Canada) Act, 1867. The expression indicates that India is a federation. The Preamble to the Constitution of India declares that the Republic of India is creation of the people of India and not of the States. But the States are also a creation of the people of India and they cannot break away from the Republic.

Although, the Republic of India is described as a union and it cannot be said to be a federation in the strict sense of the term. The Constitution makers had a purpose in choosing the word "Union" in preference to "Federation". They were of the view that the word "Union" better expresses the fact that the Union of India is not the outcome of an agreement among the old provinces with the result that it is not open to any State or a group of states to secede or withdraw from the Union or to vary the boundary of the states on their free will.

Article 1: *Name and territory of the Union*

1. India, that is Bharat, shall be a Union of States.
2. The States and the territories thereof shall be as specified in the First Schedule.
3. The territory of India shall comprise—

    a. the territories of the States;
    b. the Union territories specified in the First Schedule; and

c. such other territories as may be acquired.

According to Article 1 of the Indian Constitution, India is declared a Union of States, and the States and territories are specified in the First Schedule. The territory of India which is described in clause (3) falls under three categories— the State territories, the Union territories, the territories which may be acquired by Government of India.

Before the Constitution (Seventh Amendment) Act, 1953, the Union consisted of States which were classified into three main Categories—Parts A, B and C of the First Schedule. In addition to these there were territories specified in Past D of The First Schedule. Thus, there were four categories in all. Thus, at the time of the commencement of the Constitution (Seventh amendment) Act, 1956, the Union of India consisted of 10 Part A States, 8 Part B States, 9 Part C States and 1 Part D State.

The Constitution (Seventh Amendment) Act, 1956, has abolished the three categories and placed all the States of the Union on the same footing as a result of the reorganization made by the State Reorganization Act, 1956. At present, the territory of India consists of 29 states and 7 Union Territories.

Article 2 : Admission or establishment of new States

Parliament may by law admit into the Union, or establish, new States on such terms and conditions as it thinks fit.

The admission or establishment of a new State will be on such terms and conditions as Parliament may think fit. Such terms and conditions must, however, be consistent with the foundational principles of the basic structure of the Constitution.

Article 3 : Formation of new States and alteration of areas, boundaries or names of existing States

Parliament may by law—

a. form a new State by separation of territory from any State or by uniting two or more States or parts of States or by uniting any territory to a part of any State;

b. increase the area of any State;

c. diminish the area of any State;

d. alter the boundaries of any State;

e. alter the name of any State:

ARTICLE 12: DEFINITION OF STATE

In this Part, unless the context otherwise requires, "***the State***" includes the Government and Parliament of India and the Government and the Legislature of each of the States and all local or other authorities within the territory of India or under the control of the Government of India.

The definition of the term "State" specifies the authorities and the instrumentalities functioning within or without the territory of India which shall be deemed to be 'the State' for the purpose of Part III of the Constitution.

By the express terms of Article 12, the expression "the State" includes :

- ***the Government of India;***
- ***Parliament of India;***
- ***the Government of each of the States***
- ***the Legislature of each of the States***
- ***all local authorities within the territory of India;***
- ***all local authorities under the control of the Government of India;***
- ***all other authorities within the territory of India; and***
- ***all other authorities under the control of the Government of India.***

The State is an abstract entity and it can, therefore only act through its agencies or instrumentalities, whether such agency or instrumentality be human or juristic.

STATE INSTRUMENTALITIES - Authorities constituted under and corporations established by statutes have been held to be instrumentalities and agencies of the Government in several decisions of the Supreme Court. The observations in several of these decisions are general in nature and take into their count all instrumentalities and agencies of the State, whatever be the form which such instrumentality or agency may have assumed.

University of Madras v. Santa Bai[AIR 1954 Madras 67]

Madras High Court held that ***"other authorities"*** referred under Art.12 could only indicate authorities of a like nature i.e., ***ejusdem generis.*** If so construed or interpreted, it could only mean authorities exercising governmental or sovereign functions. It cannot include persons, natural or juristic, such as a university unless it is 'maintained by the State'

Ujjambai v. State of U.P.[AIR 1962 SC 1621]

Court rejected the above restrictive interpretation of the words "other authorities" given by the Madras High Court and held that ejusdem generis rule could not be resorted to in interpreting this expression.

Rajasthan Electricity Board v. Mohan Lal[AIR 1967 SC 1857]

Definition of State is not narrow. The expression 'other authorities' is wide enough to include all such authorities and entities that are constituted by the State under the Constitution or a statute on whom powers are conferred by law. It is not a mandate that such a statutory authority should be engaged in performing governmental or sovereign function. On this interpretation, Electricity Board, Co-operative Societies etc. which have power to make bye-laws under Co-operative Societies Act, 1911 will be included in the definition of State under Article 12.

Sukhdev v. Bhagatram[AIR 1975 SC 1331]

Oil and Natural Gas Commission, Life Insurance Corporation, Industrial Finance Corporations are all 'States' under Article 12, because all these three statutory Corporations have power to make rules and regulations for regulating conditions of service of their employees and such rules and regulations have the force of law.

Ramana Dayaram Shettyv. The International Airport Authority of India [AIR 1979 SC 1628]

The Supreme Court laid down five tests to be an *"other authority"*-

1. Entire share capital is owned or managed by State i.e. financial resources of the State is the chief funding source.
2. Enjoys monopoly status, whether it is State conferred or State protected.
3. If a department of Government is transferred to a corporation.
4. Functional character being governmental in essence i.e., if the functions of the corporation are of public importance and closely related to governmental functions.
5. Existence of deep and pervasive State control.

Ajay Hasia v. Khalid Mujib & Others[AIR 1981 SC 487]

It has been held that the societies registered under the Societies Registration Act, 1898 is an agency or instrumentality of the State and therefore it is covered under the definition of State under Article 12. The Court also observed that the test to know whether a juristic person such as registered societies is State is not how it has been brought but why it has been brought. *(i.e., the purpose behind creation of such society or trust)*

In *Union of India v. R.C. Jain* *[1981 SCR (2) 854]*, it was held that to be a *"local authority"* within the definition of "State" under Article 12, an authority must fulfil the following tests-

1. *Separate legal existence.*
2. *Function in a defined area (territory).*
3. *Has power to raise funds.*
4. *Enjoys autonomy.*
5. *Entrusted by a statute with functions which are usually entrusted to municipalities.*

WHETHER JUDICIARY ISINCLUDED IN THE DEFINITION OFSTATE???

The definition of State under Article 12 of the Constitution does not explicitly mention the Judiciary. Hence, a significant amount of controversy surrounds its status with respect to Part III of the Constitution.

Bringing the Judiciary within the scope of Article 12 would mean that it is deemed capable of acting in contravention of Fundamental Rights. It is well established that in its non-judicial functions, the Judiciary does come within the meaning of State. However, challenging a judicial decision which has achieved finality, under the writ jurisdiction of superior courts on the basis of violation of fundamental rights, remains open to debate.

Naresh v. State of Maharashtra [AIR 1967 SC 1]

The issue posed before the Supreme Court for consideration whether judiciary is covered by the expression 'State' in Article 12 of the Constitution. The Court held that the fundamental right is not infringed by the order of the Court and no writ can be issued to High Court.

This question has raised a controversy, because of non-mentioning of judiciary under Art, 12. Judiciary is the prominent organ of the State. Legislature frames the law and executor organ implements them and enjoys vast power of delegated legislation as well. One of the most important functions of Judiciary is to check invasion of fundamental rights by these two organs and their instrumentality.

Judiciary is to turn down the rules, regulation etc. which are in clear violation of fundamental rights. Inclusion of judiciary under Article 12 sets judiciary as the possible violator of fundamental rights as well. Judiciary being the guardian of the Constitution is not supposed to violate the Fundamental Rights.

Jurists like **H.M.Seervai, V.N.Shukla**consider judiciary to be State. Their view is supported by Articles 145 and 146 of the Constitution of India.

a. *The Supreme Court is empowered to make rules for regulating the practice and procedure of Courts.*

b. *The Supreme Court is empowered to make appointments of its staff and servants; decide its service conditions.*

Such kind of administrative duties of the judiciary bring it within the purview of the definition of State

<u>A.R. Antulay v. R.S. Nayak [AIR 1988 SC 1531] and N.S.Mirajkar v. State of Maharashtra[AIR1967 SC 1]</u>, it has been observed that *while exercising the rule making powers, the judiciary is covered by the expression state within Art.12 but while performing its judicial functions it is not so included.*

VII

LAWS INCONSISTENT WITH OR IN DEROGATION OF THE FUNDAMENTAL RIGHTS

ARTICLE 13

1. All laws in force in the territory of India immediately before the commencement of this Constitution, in so far as they are inconsistent with the provisions of this Part, shall, to the extent of such inconsistency, be void.

2. The State shall not make any law which takes away or abridges the rights conferred by this Part and any law made in contravention of this clause shall, to the extent of the contravention, be void.

3. In this article, unless the context otherwise requires, —

   a. "law" includes any Ordinance, order, bye-law, rule, regulation, notification, custom or usage having in the territory of India the force of law;

b. "Laws in force" includes laws passed or made by a Legislature or other competent authority in the territory of India before the commencement of this Constitution and not previously repealed, notwithstanding that any such law or any part thereof may not be then in operation either at all or in particular areas.

4. Nothing in this article shall apply to any amendment of this Constitution made under article 368.

POWER OF JUDICIAL REVIEW

The power of the Judiciary to review the Act of the Legislature or the Executive or the validity of a law or an order in order to determine its constitutional propriety and to ensure that such actions conform to the provisions of the nation's Constitution is known as the "Doctrine of Judicial Review". Judicial Review implies that the Constitution is the supreme power of the nation and all laws are under its supremacy and that any law inconsistent therewith is void through judicial review. ***Judicial reviewis adopted in the Indian Constitution from the Constitution of the United States of America.***

Judicial review has two important functions-

- Of legitimizing government action, and
- The protection of constitution against any undue encroachment by the government.

In the Indian Constitution, Judicial Review is dealt with under Article 13 which provides for the judicial review of all legislations in India, past as well as future. This power has been conferred on the High Courts and the Supreme Court of India (Article 226 and Article 32 respectively) which can declare a law unconstitutional if it is inconsistent with any of the provisions of Part III of the Constitution.

BASIS AND ORIGIN OF JUDICIAL REVIEW

The doctrine of judicial review was for the first time propounded by the Supreme Court of America. Originally, the United States Constitution did not contain an express provision for judicial review. The power of judicial review was, however, assumed by the Supreme Court of America in the historic case of ***Marbury v. Madison***by ***Justice John Marshall.***

State of Madras v. V.G. Row [AIR 1952 SC 196]

In Indian Constitution, there is an express provision for judicial review, and in this sense, it is on more solid footing than it is in America.

L. Chandra Kumar v. Union of India[AIR 1997 SC 1125]

The power of judicial review of legislative action as vested in Supreme Court by Article 32 and in High Court by Article 226 is a basic feature of the Constitution and cannot be curtailed even by constitutional amendment.

When a part of a statute is declared unconstitutional then a question arises whether the whole of the statute is to be declared void or only that part which is unconstitutional should be declared as such.

To resolve this problem, the Supreme Court has devised the doctrine of severability or separability. This doctrine means that if an offending provision can be separated from that which is unconstitutional then only that part which is offending is to be declared as void and not the entire statute. This conclusion can be very well drawn from the words that Article 13 uses i.e., *"...to theextent of such inconsistency be void"*

DOCTRINE OF SEVERABILITY

*Doctrine of Severability or Separability*is incorporated under **Art. 13 Clause (2)**which states that the State shall not make any laws which take away Fundamental Rights of a citizen. Therefore, laws made after adoption of the Constitution by the Constituent Assembly must be compatible with the Constitution, otherwise the laws and amendments will be deemed to be void-ab-initio. **Such a law willbe ultra vires**(i.e., out of authority)

When a part of the statute is declared unconstitutional, then the unconstitutional part is to be removed and the remaining valid portion will continue as valid. The idea is to retain the Act or legislation in force by discarding or deleting only the void portion and retaining the rest. However, invalid part of the law will be severed only if it is severable, i.e., if after separating the invalid part, the valid part is capable of giving effect to the legislature's intent, then only it will survive otherwise the court shall declare the entire law as invalid.

RELEVANT CASES

A.K. Gopalan v. State of Madras[AIR 1950 SC 27]

Only Section 14 of Preventive Detention Act, 1950 was held unconstitutional. Applying the doctrine of severability, whole Act except Section 14 was held valid.

State of Bombay v. F.N. Balsara[AIR 1951 SC 318]

It was observed that the certain provisions of Bombay Prohibition Act, 1949, which have been declared as void do not affect the entire statute, therefore, there is no necessity for declaring the whole statute as invalid.

Romesh Thapper v. State of Madras[AIR 1950 SC 124]

Supreme Court held that only if the unconstitutional portions cannot be removed then the whole Act will be ultra-vires and thus unconstitutional.

R.M.D.C. v. Union of India[AIR 1957 SC 628]

Supreme Court held that where after removing the invalid portion what remains constitutes a complete Code there is no necessity to declare the whole Act invalid. In such cases, whether the valid parts of the statute are separable from the invalid, the intention of the legislature is the determining factor.

THEORY OF ECLIPSE

According to ***Article 13(1)***, "All pre-constitutional laws, after the coming into force of Constitution, if in conflict with it in all or some of its provisions then the provisions of Constitution will prevail and the provisions of that pre-constitutional law will not be in force until an amendment of the Constitution relating to the same matter is made. In such situation the provision of that law will again come into force, if it is compatible with the Constitution as amended. This is called the ***Theory ofEclipse.***

Article 13(1) is prospective in nature. All pre-Constitution laws inconsistent with the Fundamental Rights will become void only after the commencement of the Constitution. They are not void ab initio.

In addition to article 13, articles 32, 124, 131, 219, 226 and 246 provide a constitutional basis tothe Judicial review in India.

CAN SUCH A LAW WHICH BECOMES UNENFORCEABLE AFTER THECONSTITUTION CAME INTO FORCE BE AGAIN REVIVED AND MADEEFFECTIVE BY AN AMENDMENT IN THE CONSTITUTION??

It was to solve this problem that the Supreme Court formulated the doctrine of eclipse in ***Bhikaji vs. State of M.P.*** [AIR 1955 SC 781]. Government of Central Province monopolized motor transport by an Act. Supreme Court held that the pre-constitutional law that violates fundamental rights is not void ab initio. It is merely eclipsed. When Art 19 was amended to allow the state to monopolize any business, the said act became constitutional again.

Post-Constitutional Laws- Clause (2) of Article 13prohibits the State to make any law which takes away or abridges the rights conferred by Part III of the Constitution. If State makes such a law, then that law will be ultra vires and void to the extent of the contravention. As contrary to Article 13 clause (1), clause (2) makes the inconsistent laws void ab initio.

Deep Chand v. State of U.P.[AIR 1959 SC 648]

It was held that doctrine of eclipse does not apply to Post-Constitutional law because such a law is void ab initio. A subsequent constitutional amendment cannot revive such a law.

State of Gujarat v. Ambica Mills[AIR 1974 SC 1300]

Overruled Deep Chand's ruling and held that a post-Constitutional law which is inconsistent with fundamental rights is not nullity or non-existent in all cases and for all purposes.

Dulare Lodh v. III Additional District Judge, Kanpur[AIR 1984 SC 1260]

Held that Doctrine of Eclipse applies to post-constitutional law and it is applicable to citizens as well.

DOCTRINE OF WAIVER

Waive means '*to give away*' or '*to surrender*'

Point of concern here regarding Part III of Indian Constitution is that whether can a citizen waivehis fundamental rights??

As held in *Behram v. State of Bombay*[AIR 1955 SC 146], the doctrine of waiver has no application to the provision of law enshrined in Part III of the Constitution of India. It is not open to an accused person to waive or give up his Constitutional rights and get convicted.

Basheshar Nath v. Income Tax Commissioner[AIR 1959 SC 149]

The appellant had reached a settlement with Income Tax Department to pay 3 Lakh rupees per month for taxes that he owed under Income Tax Act. However, later that Act was determined to be unconstitutional. So, he challenged the settlement. Income Tax Department argued that he had waived his right by reaching a settlement. Supreme Court held that, unlike USA, Indian Constitution does not follow Doctrine of Waiver. It was further held that it is not open to a citizen to waive any of the Fundamental Rights conferred by Part III of the Constitution. Fundamental rights are an obligation imposed upon the state by the Constitution. It is the court's duty to enforce them. No person can relieve the State of this obligation.

A question arises as to whether the term 'law' in Article 13 (2)includes just ordinary laws or Constitutional Amendment Actsalso.

If Constitutional Amendment Act is not covered underlaw, then the Parliament can amend the Fundamental rights byamending the Constitution itself.

For the purposes of Article 13, "*law*" is defined as including **an Ordinance, Order, bye-law, *rule, regulation, notification, custom or usage having in the territory of India the force of law.***The definition of "law" in this Article is wider than the ordinary connotation of law which refers to enacted law or enactment.

The Supreme Court in ***Shankari Prasad v. Union of India***[AIR 1951 SC **458**] held that Constitutional Amendment Act is not a law and thus Parliament can amend any Fundamental Right by using Constitutional Legislative power.

Supreme Court gave a similar verdict in ***Sajjan Singh v. State of Rajasthan*** [AIR 1965 SC 845].

In ***Golak Nath v. State of Punjab***[AIR 1967 SC 1643], the Supreme Court held that the word 'law' in Article 13 (2) included every branch of law, statutory, Constitutional, etc., and hence, if an amendment to the Constitution took away or abridged fundamental right of citizens, the amendment would be declared void.

In order to remove the difficulty created by the Supreme Court's decision in Golak Nath's case, the **Constitution (24th Amendment) Act, 1971** was enacted. By this amendment a ***new clause (4) wasadded to Article 13***which makes it clear that Constitutional amendments passed under Article 368 shall not be considered as 'law' within the meaning of Article 13 and, therefore, cannot be challenged as infringing the provisions of Part III of the Constitution. Therefore, Parliament has the power to amend Fundamental Rights through Constitutional Amendment.

The validity of Constitution (24th Amendment) Act, 1971 was challenged in the Supreme Court in ***Keshavananda Bharati v. State of Kerala***[AIR 1973 SC 1461] The Supreme Court overruled Golak Nath case and upheld the validity of 24th Amendment Act. However, the Supreme Court held that the Parliament's amendment power is limited and is subject to ***"Basic Structure"*** of the Constitution. The Supreme Court has not explicitly defined the term "Basic Structure". However, in various judgments, the Supreme Court has held that the following concepts form a part of Basic Structure-

- Supremacy of the Constitution
- Secular character of the Constitution
- Federalism
- Separation of Powers
- Power of Judicial Review
- The mandate to build a welfare state

৯৩

VIII
FUNDAMENTAL RIGHTS

Rights are claims that are essential for the existence and development of individuals. In that sense there will be a long list of rights. Whereas all these are recognized by the society, some of the most important rights are recognized by the State and enshrined in the Constitution. Such rights are called ***fundamental rights***. These rights arc fundamental because of two reasons.

1. ***These are mentioned in the Constitution which guarantees them; and***
2. ***These are justifiable, i.e., enforceable through courts.***

Being justifiable means that in case of a violation of any of the fundamental rights the individual can approach courts for their protection.

The fundamental rights were included under ***Part III of the Indian Constitution*** because they were considered essential for the development of the personality of every individual and to preserve human dignity. These Fundamental Rights guarantee to each citizen basic substantive and procedural protections from any arbitrary state actions, but some rights are enforceable against individuals. For instance, the Constitution abolishes untouchability and also prohibits begar. These provisions act as a check both on state action as well as the action of private individuals. However, these rights are not absolute or uncontrolled and are subject to reasonable restrictions as necessary for the protection of general welfare. They can also be selectively curtailed.

ORIGIN OFFUNDAMENTALRIGHTS

This Chapter of the Constitution of India is well described as the ***Magna Carta of India***. If a government enacts a law that restricts any of these rights, it will be declared invalid by courts.

As early as in 1214, the English people exacted an assurance from King John for respect of the then ancient liberties. The Magna Carta is the evidence of their success which is a written document. This is the first written document relating to fundamental rights. Thereafter from time to time, the King had to accede to many rights to his subjects. In 1689, the Bill of rights was written consolidating all important rights and liberties of the English people. In France Declaration of Rights of Man and the Citizen (1789) declared the natural, inalienable and sacred rights of man. Following the spirit of the ***Magna Carta of the British***and the ***Declaration of the Rights of Man and the Citizen of France***, the Americans incorporated the ***Bill of Rights***in their Constitution. The Americans were the first to give Bill of Rights a Constitutional status. While drafting the Constitution of India, our Constitutional draftsmen took an inspiration and therefore incorporated under Part III what is called "***fundamentalrights***"

Part III of the Indian Constitution guarantees ***six fundamental rights***to Indian citizens which are as follows:

FUNDAMENTAL RIGHTS

1. **RIGHT TO EQUALITY (Article 14 – 18)**
2. **RIGHT TO FREEDOM (Article 19 – 22)**
3. **RIGHT AGAINST EXPLOITATION (Article 23 – 24)**
4. **RIGHT TO FREEDOM OF RELIGION (Article 25 – 28)**
5. **CULTURAL AND EDUCATIONAL RIGHT (Article 29 – 30)**
6. **RIGHT TO CONSTITUTION REMEDIES (Article 32)**

The **44th Amendment**has ***abolished the right to property as a fundamental***right as ***guaranteed by Art. 19(1)(f) and Art.31 of the Constitution***. Since this Right created a lot of problems in the way of attaining the goal of socialism and equitable distribution of wealth , it was removed from the list of fundamental rights in 1978. It is not a Fundamental Right anymore.

P.D. Shamdasani v. Central Bank of India[AIR 1952 SC 59]

Bank confiscated property on loan default. Supreme Court held that fundamental rights are available against the state and not against private individuals because there already are enough safeguards under ordinary laws for such disputes.

IX
RIGHT TO EQUALITY

RIGHT TO EQUALITY [ARTICLES 14 to 18]

Right to equality is a reflection of the high aspirations as enshrined in the Preamble of the Indian Constitution. The words *"...JUSTICE, social, economic and political; EQUALITY of status and of opportunity..."* in the Preamble of the Indian Constitution gives the very backing to this essential

Article 14 to 18 guarantees the right to equality to every citizen of India. Article 14 embodies the general principles of equality before law and prohibits unreasonable discrimination between persons. The succeeding Articles 15, 16, 17 and 18 lay down specific application of the general rules laid down.

Article 14 : EQUALITY BEFORE LAW

*"The State **shall not** deny to **any person equality before the law** or the **equal protection of the laws** within the territory of India."*

The words *"**shall not**"* puts a mandatory duty upon the State not to discriminate on any ground. The words 'any person' denote that the guarantee of the equal protection of the laws is available to any person, which includes any company or association or body of individuals. The protection extends to both citizens and non-citizens and to natural persons as well as legal persons.

Article 14 uses two expressions

Equality before the law is somewhat ***negative concept*** implying the absence of any special privilege in favour of any individual and the equal subjection of all classes to the ordinary law.

Equal protection of law is a more ***positive concept*** employing equality of treatment under equal circumstances.

Thus, India has taken best aspects of both systems Unitary and federal; i.e., from England we have taken equality before the law which means supremacy of the Parliament and from America, we have taken the equal protection of the laws which means supremacy of the Courts and the law. Therefore, in India, the administration is based on a compromise between Judicial and Parliamentary Supremacy. ***This way Indian constitution aims towards establishing a rule of law.***

As Dr. Jennings puts it-

"***Equality before the law***" means that ***among equals the law should be equal and should be equally administered***, that ***like should be treated alike***. The right to sue and be sued, to prosecute and be prosecuted for the same kind of action should be same for all citizens of full age and understanding without distinctions of race, religion, wealth, social status or political influence.

It only means that **all persons similarly circumstanced shall be treated alike**, both in the privileges conferred and liabilities imposed by the laws. Equal laws should be applied to all in the same situation, and there should be no discrimination between one person and another.

Thus the rule is that the ***like should be treated alike*** and not that unlike should be treated alike

The guarantee of equality before the law is an aspect of what Dicey calls the rule of the law in England. It means that no man is above the law and that every person, whatever be his rank or conditions, is subject to the jurisdiction of ordinary courts. Rule of law requires that no person shall be subjected to harsh, uncivilized or discriminatory treatment even when the object is the securing of the paramount exigencies of law and order.

PROFESSOR DICEY GAVE THREE MEANINGS OF THE RULE OF LAW

1. Supremacy of the law

2. Equality before the law

3. Predominance of law

The Constitution is the result of the ordinary law of the land It means that the source of the right of individual is not the written Constitution but the rules as defined and enforced by the courts.

ART. 14 PERMITS REASONABLE CLASSIFICATION BUT ITPROHIBITS CLASS LEGISLATION

What **_Article 14 forbids is class legislation_**and **_it does not forbid reasonable classification._**The classification must not be "arbitrary, artificial or evasive" but must be based on some real and substantial bearing, a just and reasonable relation to the object sought to be achieved by the legislation.

Class legislation is that which makes an improper discrimination by conferring particular privileges upon a class of persons arbitrarily selected from a large number of persons, all of whom stand in the same relation to the privilege granted and that no reasonable distinction or substantial difference can be found justifying the inclusion of one and the exclusion of the other from such privilege.

From the very nature of society there should be different laws in different places and the legislature controls the policy and enacts laws in the best interest of the safety and security of the state. In fact identical treatment in unequal circumstances would amount to inequality. So, a reasonable classification is not only permitted but it is necessary if society is to progress.

Classification to be reasonable must fulfil the following two conditions:-

⦿ **_Firstly, the classification must be founded on the intelligible differentia._**

⦿ **_Secondly, the differentia must have a rational relation to the objectsought or to be achieved by the act._**

The differentia which is the basis of the classification and the object of the act are two distinct things. What is necessary is that **there must be nexus between the basis of classification and theobject of the Act which makes the classification.**It is only when there is no reasonable basis for a classification that legislation making such classification may be declared discriminatory and violative of Article 14.

NEWCONCEPTOFEQUALITY

E.P. Royappa v. State of Tamil Nadu[AIR 1974 SC 555]

Supreme Court challenges the traditional concept of equality which was based on reasonable classification and has laid down a new concept of equality. The Honourable Judges who gave the decision were of the opinion that "Equality is a dynamic concept with many aspects and dimensions and it cannot be cabined or confined within traditional limits".

D.S Nakara v. union of India[AIR 1983 SC 130]

In this case, Supreme Court struck down Rule 34 of the Central Services (Pension) Rules, 1972 as unconstitutional on the ground that the classification made by it between pensioners retiring before a certain date and retiring after that date was not based on the any rational principle and it was arbitrary and violative of Article 14 of Indian Constitution.

Mithu v. State of Punjab[AIR 1983 SC 473]

The Supreme Court struck down ***Section 303 of Indian Penal Code***as unconstitutional on the ground that the classification between persons who commits murders whilst under the sentence of imprisonment and those who commit murders whilst they were not under the sentence of life imprisonment for the purposes of making the sentence of death mandatory in the case of the former class and optional in the latter class was not based on any rational principle and was somehow violative of Article 14.

K.A. Abbas v. Union of India[AIR 1971 SC 481]

Validity of Cinematograph Act, 1952 was challenged on the ground that it makes unreasonable classification of cinema films in "U" films and "A" films. Supreme Court held the classification to be logical and a reasonable one as also not being violative of Article 14 in any manner.

Air India v. Nargesh Meerza[AIR 1981 SC 1829]

Supreme Court struck down the Air India and Indian Airlines Regulations on the retirement and pregnancy bar on services of air hostesses as unconstitutional on the ground that the conditions laid down therein were entirely unreasonable and arbitrary. *Regulation46* of Indian Airlines Regulations provided that an air hostess would retire from the service upon attaining the age of 35 years or on marriage, if it took place within 4 years of service or on first pregnancy, whichever occur earlier. Such rules for the termination of service on pregnancy were manifestly unreasonable and arbitrary as it was in violation of Article 14 of Indian Constitution.

Randhir Singh v. Union of India[AIR 1982 SC 879]

Supreme Court held that although the principle of 'equal pay for equal work' is not expressly declared by our Constitution to be a fundamental right, but it is certainly a Constitutional goal under Article 14. This right can, therefore, be enforced in cases of unequal scales of pay based on irrational classification.

Javed v. State of Haryana[AIR 2003 SC 3057]

Petitioners challenged the validity of Section 175 (1) (g) of the Haryana Panchayati Raj Act, 1994 on the ground that it was violative of Article 14 as the said provision disqualified a person having more than two children from contesting elections for Sarpanch or Panch in Gram Panchayats. Supreme Court upheld the constitutionality of the said provision and held that it is not violating Article 14 in any manner.

Article 15: Prohibition of discrimination on grounds of religion, race, caste, sex or place of birth

1. The State shall not discriminate against any citizen on grounds only of religion, race, caste, sex, place of birth or any of them. **{rrcsp}**
2. No citizen shall, on grounds only of religion, race, caste, sex, place of birth or any of them, be subject to any disability, liability, restriction or condition with regard to—

   a. access to shops, public restaurants, hotels and places of public entertainment; or
   b. the use of wells, tanks, bathing ghats, roads and places of public resort maintained wholly or partly out of State funds or dedicated to the use of the general public.

3. Nothing in this article shall prevent the State from making any special provision for women and children.
4. Nothing in this article or in clause (2) of Article 29 shall prevent the State from making any special provision for the advancement of any socially and educationally backward classes of citizens or for the Scheduled Castes and the Scheduled Tribes.
5. Nothing in this article or in sub-clause (g) of clause (1) of article 19 shall prevent the State from making any special provision, by law, for the advancement of any socially and educationally backward classes of citizens or for the Scheduled Castes or the Scheduled Tribes in so far as such special provisions relate to their admission to educational institutions including private educational institutions, whether aided or unaided by the State, other than the minority educational institutions referred to in clause (1) of article 30.

Article 15 provides for a particular application of the general principle embodied under Article

14. ***The guarantee under Article 15 is available to citizens only***. The state cannot discriminate only on the above-mentioned grounds but can discriminate on grounds other than these. The rights under 15 (2) are not only available against a State but also against other citizens.

Article 15 (1) states that no citizen shall be discriminated only on the grounds of religion, race, caste, sex, place of birth or any of them. But there are special considerations for women and children, SC/ST, OBC. Exceptions for these categories are mentioned in Clause (2) and (3) of Article 15. ***Article 15 (2)***is a specific application of the general prohibition contained in Article 15 (1).

While Clause (1) prohibits discrimination by the State; clause (2) prohibits both the State and private individuals from making any discrimination.

Women and children require special treatment on account of their very nature and therefore ***Article 15 (3)***empowers the ***State to make special provisions for women and children***. The reason is that "women's physical structure and the performance of maternal functions place her at a disadvantage in the struggle for subsistence and her physical well-being. Thus, under Article 42, women workers can be given special maternity relief and a law to this effect will not infringe Article 15 (1). Also, if an educational institution is established by the State exclusively for women or if reservation of seats is made for women in a college, it does not offend Article 15 (1).

Article 15 Clause (4)is another exception to clause (1) and (2) of Article 15. Article 15(4) has been inserted by the constitution (first amendment) Act, 1951.

It was ***added by the Constitution (1st Amendment) Act, 1951***, as a result of the decision in ***State of Madras v.Champakam Dorairajan***[AIR 1951 SC 226]. The provision made in clause (4) is only an enabling provision and does not impose any obligation on the State to take any special action under it. It merely confers discretion to act if necessary by way of making special provision for backward classes. A writ cannot be issued to the State to make reservation. The basic principle underlying this clause is that a preferential treatment can be given validly where socially and educationally backward classes need it.

Thus under Article 15 (4), two things are to be determined-

1. Who are socially and educationally backward classes?
2. What is the limit of reservation?

Constitution nowhere defines 'backward classes'. **_Article 340,_** however, empowers the President to appoint a Commission to investigate conditions of socially and educationally backward classes. On the basis of the report of the Commission the president may specify who are to be considered as 'Backward classes'. In **_Balaji v. State of Mysore_**[AIR 1963 SC 649], it was held that 'backward' and 'more backward' classification is not bad.

In the historic **_Mandal Commission Case [Indira Sawhney v. Union of India, AIR 2000 SC498]_**, the Supreme Court by 6-3 majority has held that the sub-classification of backward classes into backward into more backward and backward classes for the purpose of Article 16(4) can be done. But as result of sub-classification, the reservation cannot exceed more than 50 percent. Creamy layer must be excluded from the backward classes.

High caste girl marrying a male of Scheduled tribe is not entitled to reservation benefit under Clause (4) of Article 15. Also, a Scheduled Caste or a Scheduled Tribe candidate is entitled to reservation benefit only in the State of his origin and not in other State where he migrates to.

Article 15 clause (5)- In order to serve the educationally and socially backward classes, the State asked the private education institutions also to reserve seats for the backward classes. Private institutions objected to it, stating it would amount to violation of right under Article 19 (1) (g). The Parliament, by amending the Constitution in 2005, added Clause (5) to Article 15. According to this, it is mandatory to reserve seats for backward classes also even in private institutions whether aided or unaided, by the State. The only exception is educational institutions run by minority communities. A law was enacted in this effect called Central Educational Institutions Reservation in Admission Act, 2006. This Act was challenged in the Supreme Court, but the Supreme Court upheld the validity of this law.

Landmark cases on Clause (5)-

- **_T.M. Pai Foundation v. State of Karnataka_** [AIR 2003 SC 355]
- **_Islamic Academy v. State of Karnataka_** [AIR 2003 SC 3724]
- **_P. A. Inamdar v. State of Maharashtra_** [AIR 2005 SC 3226]

ARTICLE 16: EQUALITY OF OPPORTUNITYIN MATTERS OF PUBLIC EMPLOYMENT

1. There shall be equality of opportunity for all citizens in matters relating to employment or appointment to any office under the State.
2. No citizen shall, on grounds only of religion, race, caste, sex, descent, place of birth, residence or any of them, be ineligible for, or discriminated against in respect of, any employment or office under the State.
3. Nothing in this article shall prevent Parliament from making any law prescribing, in regard to a class or classes of employment or appointment to an office under the Government of, or any local or other authority within, a State or Union territory, any requirement as to residence within that State or Union territory prior to such employment or appointment.
4. Nothing in this article shall prevent the State from making any provision for the reservation of appointments or posts in favour of any backward class of citizens which, in the opinion of the State, is not adequately represented in the services under the State.

(4A) Nothing in this article shall prevent the State from making any provision for reservation in matters of promotion, with consequential seniority, to any class or classes of posts in the services under the State in favour of the Scheduled Castes and the Scheduled Tribes which, in the opinion of the State, are not adequately represented in the services under the State.

(4B) Nothing in this article shall prevent the State from considering any unfilled vacancies of a year which are reserved for being filled up in that year in accordance with any provision for reservation made under clause (4) or clause (4A) as a separate class of vacancies to be filled up in any succeeding year or years and such class of vacancies shall not be considered together with the vacancies of the year in which they are being filled up for determining the ceiling of fifty per cent. reservation on total number of vacancies of that year.

5. Nothing in this article shall affect the operation of any law which provides that the incumbent of an office in connection with the affairs of any religious or denominational institution or any member of the governing body thereof shall be a person professing a particular religion or belonging to a particular denomination.

__Article 16 (1) and (2) applies only in respect of employment or office under the State.Clause (3), (4), (4-A), (4-B), (5) of Article 16 provide four exceptions to this general rule ofequality of opportunity.__

__*Clause (4)*__enables the State to make provision for the reservation of posts in government jobs in favour of any backward class of citizen which, in the opinion of the State, is not adequately represented in the services of the State.

The newly added __*clause (4-A), added by 77th Amendment, 1955,*__ empowers the __*State tomake any provision for the reservation in matters of promotions of SCs and STs*__which, in the opinion of the State, are not adequately represented in the services of the State.

__*The Constitution (81st Amendment) Act, 2000*__ has added a new __*clause (4-B)*__in Article 16 which seeks __*to end the 50% limit for Scheduled Castes and Scheduled Tribes and other BackwardClasses in backlog vacancies*__which could be filled up due to the non-availability of eligible candidates of these categories in the previous year or years.

__*Important Amendments with reference to Article 16 are 77th, 81st, 85th Constitutional Amendments.*__

ARTICLE 17: ABOLITION OF UNTOUCHABILITY

"Untouchability" is abolished and its practice in any form is forbidden. The enforcement of any disability arising out of __*"Untouchability" shall be an offence*__punishable in accordance with law.

In exercise of the powers conferred by Article 35, Parliament has enacted the Untouchability (Offences) Act, 1955. This Act was amended by the Untouchability (Offences) Amendment Act, 1976, in order to make the law more stringent to remove untouchability from the society. It has now been renamed as '__*The Protection of Civil Rights Act, 1955*__'. Under the amended Act, any discrimination on the ground of untouchability will be considered as an offence.

ARTICLE 18: ABOLITION OF TITLES

1. No title, not being a military or academic distinction, shall be conferred by the State.
2. No citizen of India shall accept any title from any foreign State.

3. No person who is not a citizen of India shall, while he holds any office of profit or trust under the State, accept without the consent of the President any title from any foreign State.

4. No person holding any office of pofit or trust under the State shall, without the consent of the President, accept any present, emolument, or office of any kind from or under any foreign State.

Article 18 prohibits the State to confer titles on anybody whether a citizen or a non-citizen. Military and academic distinctions are, however, exempted from the prohibition. Clause (3) is there to ensure loyalty to the Government that such person serves for the time being and to shut out all foreign influence in Government affairs or administration.

This is the reason why the conferment of titles of "Bharat Ratna", "Padma Vibhushan", "Padma Shri", etc. is not prohibited under Article 18 as they merely denote State recognition of good work or exceptional or distinguished services of the high integrity by citizens in any field.

These National Awards were formally instituted in January, 1954 by two Presidential Notifications. The said Notifications also provide that any person without distinction of race, occupation, position or sex, shall be eligible for these awards. It was also made clear that these civilian awards cannot be used as titles and should not be attached as suffixes or prefixes to the name. In 1977, these awards were discontinued but were again revived in 1980. Since then, the National Awards are conferred annually on Republic Day.

X

RIGHT TO FREEDOM

<u>RIGHT TOFREEDOM[ARTICLES 19 to 22]</u>

Personal liberty is the most important of all fundamental rights. ***Articles 19 to 22*** deal with different aspects of this basic right. The rights guaranteed under Article 19 are available only to citizens and not to an alien or a foreigner. Citizens under Article 19 mean only natural persons and not legal or juristic persons, such as corporation or a company which cannot claim a right under Article 19 because they are not natural persons.

<u>**Art. 19 (1)(a)**</u> **Freedom of Speech and Expression**

<u>**Art. 19 (1)(b)**</u> **Freedom to assemble peacefully and without arms**

<u>**Art. 19 (1)(c)**</u> **Freedom to form associations and unions**

<u>**Art. 19 (1)(d)**</u> **Freedom to move freely throughout the territory of India**

<u>**Art. 19 (1)(e)**</u> **Freedom to reside and settle in any part of India**

<u>**Art. 19 (1)(g)**</u> **Freedom to practise any profession or**

to carry on any occupation, trade or business

The purpose of providing these freedoms is to build and maintain an environment for proper functioning of democracy. However, ***<u>these six freedoms are not absolute.</u>***The guarantee of each of the above rights is, therefore, restricted by the Constitution itself by conferring upon the State to impose certain ***reasonable restrictions***on each of them as may be necessary in the larger interest of the community. ***<u>The restrictions on these freedoms are provided in clauses (2) to (6) of Article 19of the Constitution.</u>***

ARTICLE 19 (2) This provide reasonable restriction and <u>*8 Grounds namely-*</u>

1. Security of the State

2. Friendly relations with Foreign States
3. Public order
4. Decency or Morality
5. Contempt of Court
6. Defamation
7. Incitement of an offence
8. Sovereignty and integrity of India

The restrictions on the rights under Article 19 (1) can only be imposed by a 'Law' and not executive or departmental instructions. Restrictions should not be arbitrary or of an excessive nature, beyond what is actually required in the interest of the public. It is the Courts and not the Legislature which has to decide finally whether a restriction is reasonable or not.

FREEDOM OF SPEECH AND EXPRESSION[ARTICLE 19(1) (a)]

In ***Romesh Thapar v. State of Madras***[AIR 1950 SC 124], Patanjali Shastri, Justice observed: *"Freedom of speech and of the press lay at the foundation of all democratic organisations, for without free political discussion no public education, so essential for the proper functioning of the process of popular government, is possible."*

Territorial extent of freedom- In a landmark judgement of ***Maneka Gandhi v. Union of India***[AIR 1978 SC 597], the Supreme Court held that the freedom of speech and expression has no geographical limitation and it carries with it the right of a citizen to gather information and to exchange thought with others not only in India but abroad also.

RIGHT TO VOTE

The Supreme Court observed in ***Union of India v. Association for Democratic Reforms***- "One sided information, disinformation, misinformation and non-information, all equally create an uninformed citizenry which makes democracy a farce. Freedom of speech and expression includes right to impart and receive information which includes that voters have a right to know about their candidates and also freedom to hold opinions".

Bijoe Emmaneul v. State of Kerala[(1986)3 SCC 615]

The Supreme Court held that no person can be compelled to sing National Anthem, "if he has genuine conscientious objections based on religious faith". Standing up respectfully while the National Anthem is being sung is good enough as freedom under Art. 19 (1) (a) also includes freedom of silence.

***Secretary, Minister of I & B v. Cricket Association of Bengal* [(1995)2 SCC 161]**

Government has no monopoly on the electronic media and a citizen has under Article 19(1), a right to telecast and broadcast to the viewers/listeners through electronic media any important event. The Government can impose restrictions on such a right only on grounds specified in Clause (2) of Article 19 and not on any other ground.

***Tata Press Ltd. v. Mahanagar Telephone Nigam Ltd.* [(1995) 5 SCC 139] & *Hamdard Dawakhana v. Union of India*[AIR 1960 SC 554]**

Commercial advertisement also forms a part of freedom of speech and expression. Commercial speech cannot be denied the protection of Article 19(1) (a) merely because the same are issued by businessmen.

***People's Union for Civil Liberties v. Union of India*[AIR 1997 SC 568]**

Telephone tapping is an invasion on right to privacy.

FREEDOM OF THE PRESS

The phrase, "freedom of press" has not been used in Article 19, but freedom of expression includes freedom of press. Freedom of press is implied from Article 19(1)(a) of the Constitution. Thus, the press is subject to the restrictions that are provided under the Article 19(2) of the Constitution.

Before Independence, there was no Constitutional or statutory provision to protect the freedom of press. The Preamble of the Indian Constitution ensures to all its citizens the liberty of expression.

Freedom of the press has been included as part of freedom of speech and expression under the Article 19 of the Universal Declarations of Human Rights. The heart of Article 19 says: "Everyone has the right to freedom of opinion and expression, this right includes freedom to hold opinions without interference and to seek, receive and impart information and ideas through any media and regardless of frontiers."

***Indian Express Newspapers v. Union of India*[(1985) 1 SCC 641]**

It has been held that the press plays a very significant role in the democratic machinery. The courts have duty to uphold the freedom of press and invalidate all laws and administrative actions that abridge that freedom. Freedom of press has three essential elements.

1. ***Freedom of access to all sources of information,***
2. ***Freedom of publication, and***
3. ***Freedom of circulation.***

There are instances when the freedom of press has been suppressed by the legislature. The authority of the government, in such circumstances, has been under the scanner of judiciary. In the case of ***Brij Bhushan v. State of Delhi***(AIR 1950 SC 129), the validity of censorship previous to the publication (***pre-censorship***) of an English Weekly of Delhi, the Organiser was questioned. The court struck down the Section 7 of the East Punjab Safety Act, 1949, which directed the editor and publisher of a newspaper "to submit for scrutiny, in duplicate, before the publication, till the further orders, all communal matters all the matters and news and views about Pakistan, including photographs, and cartoons", on the ground that it was a restriction on the liberty of the press. Similarly, prohibiting newspaper from publishing its own views or views of correspondents about a topic has been held to be a serious encroachment on the freedom of speech and expression.

Romesh Thapar v. State of Madras[AIR 1950 SC 124]

Entry and circulation of the English journal "Cross Road", printed and published in Bombay, was banned by the Government of Madras. The same was held to be violative of the freedom of speech and expression, as "without liberty of circulation, publication would be of little value".

Prabha Dutt v. Union of India[AIR 1982 SC 6]

The Supreme Court directed the Superintendent of Tihar Jail to allow representatives of a few newspapers to interview Ranga and Billa, the death sentence convicts, as they wanted to be interviewed.

Sakal Papers Ltd. v. Union of India[AIR 1962 SC 305]

The Daily Newspapers (Price and Page) Order, 1960, which fixed the number of pages, size and the price in which a newspaper could be published challenged as unconstitutional being violative of freedom of press and not a reasonable restriction under the Article 19(2). It was held that the right under Article 19 cannot be curtailed with the object of placing restrictions on the business activity of a citizen.

Bennett Coleman and Company v. Union of India[AIR 1973 SC 106]

The validity of the Newsprint Control Order, which fixed the maximum number of pages, was struck down by the Supreme Court of India holding it to be violative of provision of Article 19(1)(a) and not to be reasonable restriction under Article 19(2). The Court struck down the rebuttal of the Government that it would help small newspapers to grow.

R. Rajagopal v. State of Tamil Nadu (Known as 'Auto Shankar Case')[(1994) 6 SCC 632]

Supreme Court held that Government has no authority in law to impose a prior-restraint upon publication of defamatory material against its officials. It was held that no action could be initiated against the press if the publication was based on public records including Court records.

K.A. Abbas v. Union of India[AIR 1971 SC 481]

This is the first case where the question whether prior censorship of films under Cinematograph Act, 1952 is included in Article 19(2) came for the consideration of the Supreme Court. Court held that the censorship and categorisation of films into 'U' and 'A' category was reasonable and justified.

Ranjit D. Udeshi v. State of Maharashtra[AIR 1965 SC 881]

The word 'obscenity' of English law is identical with the word 'indecency' under the Indian Constitution. In an English case of _R. v. Hicklin_, the test was laid down according to which it is seen 'whether the tendency of the matter charged as obscene tend to deprave and corrupt the minds which are open to such immoral influences'. This test was upheld by the Supreme Court in Ranjit D. Udeshi case. In this case the Court upheld the conviction of a book seller who was prosecuted under Section 292, Indian Penal code, for selling and keeping the book _Lady Chatterley's Lover_. The standard of morality varies from time to time and from place to place.

FREEDOM TO ASSEMBLE PEACEFULLY ANDWITHOUT ARMS [ARTICLE 19 (1) (b)]

Article 19(1)(b) guarantees to all citizens of India right to assemble peacefully and without arms. The right of assembly also includes right to hold meetings and to take out processions. This right is subject to following restrictions-

1. The assembly must be peaceful
2. It must be unarmed
3. Reasonable restrictions can be imposed under Clause 3 of Article 19

_**Chapter VIII of the Indian Penal code, 1860**_lays down the conditions when an assembly becomes "unlawful". Under _**Sec. 141**_of the IPC, an assembly of five or more persons becomes an unlawful assembly if the common object of the person's composing assembly is-

1. To resist the execution of any law or legal process,
2. To commit any mischief or criminal trespass
3. Obtaining possession of any property by force

4. To compel a person to do what he is not legally bound to do or omit which he is legally entitled to do.

5. To overawe the Government by means of criminal force or show of criminal force or any public servant in the exercise of his lawful powers.

Freedom to assemble peacefully without arms can be reasonably restricted by the State in the interest of public order and the sovereignty and integrity of India.

FREEDOM TO RESIDE AND SETTLE IN ANY PART OF THETERRITORY OF INDIA[ARTICLE 19 (1) (e)]

Freedom to reside and settle in any part of the territory of India is also subject to reasonable restrictions by the State in the interest of the general public or for the protection of the scheduled tribes because certain safeguards as are envisaged here seem to be justified to protect indigenous and tribal peoples from exploitation and coercion. *Article 370* restricts citizens from other Indian states and Kashmiri women who marry men from other states from purchasing land or property in Jammu & Kashmir.

FREEDOM TO PRACTICE ANY PROFESSION OR TO CARRY ON ANY OCCUPATION, TRADE OR BUSINESS[ARTICLE 19 (1) (g)]

The State may impose reasonable restrictions in the interest of the general public on this right. Thus, there is no right to carry on a business which is dangerous or immoral. Also, professional or technical qualifications may be prescribed for practicing any profession or carrying on any trade.

Sodan singh v. New Delhi Municipal Committee[AIR 1989 SC 1988]

Supreme Court held that the hawkers have a fundamental right to carry on trade on pavement of roads, but subject to reasonable restrictions under article 19 Clause (6).

ARTICLE 20 :PROTECTION IN RESPECT OF CONVICTION FOR OFFENCES

Article 20 affords protection against arbitrary and excessive punishment to any person who commits an offence.

1. No person shall be convicted of any offence except for violation of the law in force at the time of the commission of the act charged as an offence, nor be subjected to a penalty greater than that which might have been inflicted under the law in force at the time of the commission of the

offence

[Protection against Ex post facto law] This has two basic implications-

a. **_A person can be convicted of an offence only if he has violated a law in force at the time when he is alleged to have committed the offence._**
b. **_No person can be subjected to a greater penalty than what might have been given to him under the law that was prevalent when he committed the offence._**

2. No person shall be prosecuted and punished for the same offence more than once.

[Protection against Double jeopardy]

3. No person accused of any offence shall be compelled to be a witness against himself.

[Prohibition against self-incrimination]

According to Article 20(1), **_no one can be awarded punishment which is more than what the law of the land prescribes at that time._** This legal axiom is based on the principle that no criminal law can be made retrospective, that is, for an act to become an offence, the essential condition is that it should have been an offence legally at the time of committing it.

Protection against double jeopardy- Article 20(2) establishes what is known as "principle of double jeopardy", that is, no person can be convicted twice for the same offence. This principle was first established in the Magna Carta. This clause embodies the common law rule of '**_nemo debet vis vexari pro una et eadem causa_**' which means that no man should be put twice in peril for the same offence. If he is prosecuted again for the same offence for which he has already been prosecuted he can take complete defence of his former acquittal or conviction.

Prohibition against self-incrimination

As per Article 20(3), no person accused of any offence shall be compelled to be a witness against himself. "Compulsion" in this article refers to what in law is called "Duress" (injury, beating or unlawful imprisonment to make a person do something that he does not want to do). This article is known as a safeguard against self incrimination.

Self-incriminationis the act of exposing oneself (generally, by making a statement) "to an accusation or charge of crime; to involve oneself or another person in a criminal prosecution or the danger thereof."

Self-incrimination can occur either directly or indirectly:

- ***directly***, by means of interrogation where information of a self-incriminatory nature is disclosed;
- ***indirectly***, when information of a self-incriminatory nature is disclosed voluntarily without pressure from another person.

Relevant Cases-
State of Bombay v. Kathi Kalu[AIR 1961 SC 108]
Nandani Satpathy v. PL Dani[AIR 1977 SC 1025]

NARCO ANALYSIS, POLYGRAPHY, BRAINMAPPING AND FINGER PRINTING

Selvi v. State of Karnataka [AIR 2010 SC 1974]

People on whom this test is conducted often allege it to be violation of their right to self- incrimination guaranteed under Article 20(3) of the Constitution of India.

What is Narco Analysis test?

Narco-Analysis test, also known as '***Truth Serum Test***', is done with the main intent and aim of extracting information from the accused when he is in hypnotic state. The Hon'ble Supreme Court of India is of the view that narco analysis, polygraph or brain mapping tests cannot be conducted on any person, whether an accused or a suspect, without their consent.

The Court further stresses that no person should be compelled to go through such test as it amounts to violation of Art 21 i.e. Right to Personal Liberty and prohibits self-incrimination and thereby violates Art 20 (3). In short according to Supreme Court, conducting Narco Analysis Test is Unconstitutional and Illegal.

PROTECTION OF LIFE ANDPERSONAL LIBERTY[ARTICLE 21]

"No person shall be deprived of his life or personal libertyexcept according to procedure established by law."

This means that a person's life and personal liberty can only be disputed if that person has committed a crime. However, the right to life does not include the right to die, and hence, suicide or an attempt thereof, is an offence.

"Personal liberty" includes all the freedoms which are not included in Article 19 (that is, the six freedoms). The right to travel abroad is also covered under "personal liberty" in Article 21.

*The words "**No person...**" simply indicates that this right is available to every individual, be it a citizen or a non- citizen.* **The right guaranteed in Article 21 is available to 'citizens' as well as 'non-citizens'.**

"..procedure established by law.."

Constitution make no distinction between a law made by the legislature & ordinance issued by president, both are equally subject to limitation which the Constitution has placed upon that power i.e. **"..procedure established by law."**

It extends both to substantive as well as procedural laws. A procedure not fulfilling these attributes is no procedure at all in the eyes of art.21

In **American Constitution**, the corresponding provision is-

SCOPE OF THE RIGHT UNDER ARTICLE 21

"No person shall be deprived of his life or liberty or propertyexcept by due process of law"

Here, '..**due process..**' refers to a *just, fair and a reasonable procedure.*

A.K. Gopalan v. State of Madras[1950 SC 27]

A communist leader A. K. Gopalan was detained under Preventive Detention Act, 1950. The first major constitutional issue came out of the preventive detention of communist leader A. K. Gopalan. The issue was whether somebody's detention could be justified merely on the ground that it had been carried out "according to the procedure established by law," as stipulated in Article 21 of the Constitution. Or, would that procedure be valid only if it complied with principles of natural justice such as giving a hearing to the affected person?

In this case, the Supreme Court, taking a narrow view of Article 21, refused to consider if the procedure established by law suffered from any deficiencies. Three decades later, Supreme Court took a new approach on this issue in the Maneka Gandhi case of 1978. The provocation was the arbitrary law that had allowed the Janata Party government to take away

Maneka's passport without any remedy. Importing the American concept of due process, the Supreme Court ruled that the procedure established by law for depriving somebody of their life or personal liberty had to be "just, fair and reasonable".

Kharak Singh v. State of U.P.[AIR 1963 SC 1295]

UP Police performed domiciliary visits to make sure that he was at home in the nights. This was challenged. SC held the following-

1. Personal liberty is not confined only to bodily restraint or confinement in prisons but includes all those things through which life is enjoyed.
2. Personal Liberty means much more that mere animal existence.
3. Article 19 gives some of the freedoms required to enjoy personal liberty, while Article 21 constitutes the rest.
4. Since there was no law which could justify domiciliary visits, they were held to be an unauthorized intrusion into a person's life and were held to be in violation of Article 21.

Maneka Gandhi v. Union of India[AIR 1978 SC 597]

Prior to Maneka Gandhi's decision, Article 21 guaranteed the right to life and personal liberty to citizens only against arbitrary action of the executive, and not from legislative action. But after this case Article 21 now protects the right to life and personal liberty of citizen not only from the executive action but from the legislative action also.

Facts :Maneka Gandhi's passport was impounded by the Central government under the Passport Act in the interest of the general public and in the name of security reasons. Maneka filed a writ petition challenging the order on the ground of violation of fundamental right of personal liberty under Article

21. The major ground of challenge was the order impounding the passport was null and void as it had been made without affording her an opportunity of being heard in her defence. Also, that such an impounding order was not in accordance with the procedure established by law.

After Maneka Gandhi's case, there has been a new interpretation of this right. Earlier the concept as understood was that Article 21 gives a safeguard only against executive action which is unsupported by law. In this case, the Supreme Court made it clear that a _**procedure established by thelegislature must also be reasonable, just and fair and not an arbitrary one. In order that the procedure was just, fair and reasonable, it should conform to the principles**_ *of natural justice.*

The Constituent Assembly in 1948 eventually omitted the phrase "due process" in favour of "procedure established by law". As a result, Article 21, which prevents the encroachment of life or personal liberty by the State except in accordance with the procedure established by law, was, until 1978, construed narrowly as being restricted to executive action. However, in 1978, the Supreme Court in the case of *Maneka Gandhi v. Union of India* extended the protection of Article 21 to legislative action, holding that any law laying down a procedure must be just, fair and reasonable, and effectively reading due process into Article 21. In the same case, the Supreme Court also ruled that "life" under Article 21 meant more than a mere "animal existence"; it would include the right to live with human dignity and all other aspects which made life "meaningful, complete and worth living". Subsequent judicial interpretation has broadened the scope of Article 21 to include within it a number of rights including those to livelihood, clean environment, good health, speedy trial and humanitarian treatment while imprisoned. The right to education at elementary level has been made one of the Fundamental Rights under Article 21A by the 86th Constitutional amendment of 2002.

Francis Coralie v. Union territory of Delhi[AIR 1981 SC 746]

Right to life is not only about mere animal existence rather it means something more than just physical survival. It rather involves many other basic rights which are necessary to lead a life with human dignity.

People's Union for Democratic Rights v. Union of India[AIR 1982 SC 1473]

It was held that if the government fails to ensure the proper implementation of the labour laws, it is a deemed denial of the right to life and personal liberty of the workers.

Bandhua Mukti Morcha v. UoI[AIR 1984 SC 802]

Supreme Court held that right to life should be taken to mean right to live with human dignity free from exploitation.

Neerja Choudhary v. State of M.P.[AIR 1984 SC 1099]

It was held that bonded labourers should not only be identified and released but also they must be rehabilitated after their release.

Parmanand Katara v. Union of India[AIR 1989 SC 2039]

SC held that it is the professional duty of all doctors, whether government or private, to extend medical aid to the injured persons so as to preserve his life without waiting for the compliance of the legal formalities like form filling etc.

M.C. Mehta v. Union of India[AIR 1988 SC 1115]

SC held that a pollution free environment i.e. pure air, pure water, edible food do form an essential part of right to life.

Subhash Kumar v. State of Bihar[AIR 1991 SC 420]

Right to pollution free air and water falls within the ambit of Article 21.

Indian Council for Enviro Legal Action v. Union of India[(1996)3 SCC 212]

Private companies are also bound under statutes and under constitution not to affect the right to life of the citizens.

Vellore Citizens Welfare Forum v. Union of India[(1996)5 SCC 650]

Precautionary principle and polluter pays principal have been accepted as part of the law of land. *"Green benches"* have been formed in pursuance of these two principles. Thus the two concepts aim towards ensuring a pollution free atmosphere and creates an extra burden on the private companies and factories etc to be have more self monitoring mechanisms towards ensuring rights of the citizens.

Olga Tellis V. Bombay Municipal Corporation[AIR 1986 SC 180]

The right to livelihood is borne out of the right to life, as no person can live without the means of living, that is, the means of livelihood. If the right to livelihood is not treated as a part and parcel of the Constitutional right to life, the easiest way of depriving a person of his right to life would be deprived him of means of livelihood to the point of abrogation.

Murali S. Deora v. Union of India[AIR 2002 SC 40]

Smoking in public places was banned. By no means, the passive smokers must be allowed to get affected by the act of a active smoker. It was here when smoking in public places such as auditoriums, hospital buildings, health institutions or hospitals, educational institutions, libraries, court buildings, public offices, public conveyances including railways, is banned.

People's Union for Civil Liberties(PUCL) v. Union of India[AIR 1997 SC 568]

Popularly known as *"Phone Tapping case"*. Supreme Court held that telephone tapping is a serious invasion of an individual's right to privacy which is a part of the right to life and personal liberty and it should not be resorted by the State unless there is public emergency or interest of public safety requires.

Sheela Barse v. State of Maharashtra[(1983) 2 SCC 96]

Supreme Court held that the use of 'third degree' method by police is violative of Article 21.

Vishakha v. State of Rajasthan[AIR 1997 SC 3011]

The SC has declared sexual harassment of a working woman at her place of work as amounting to violation of rights of gender equality and right to life and liberty which is clear violation of Article 14, 15 and 21. In this case, the Supreme Court has formulated the basic guidelines as to the conditions of work of working women at their work places and factories etc. The guidelines basically relates to the number of working hours and the phase of work i.e. the female workers can only work in between 8 A.M. to 5 P.M.

Hussainara Khatoon v. State of Bihar[AIR 1979 SC 1360]

Right to speedy trial was recognised to be a part of Art. 21

A.R. Antulay v. R.S. Nayak[AIR 1988 SC 1531]

The SC laid down detailed guidelines for speedy trials of an accused in a criminal trial. However, the SC declined to fix any time limit for trial of offences. The Court held that the right to speedy trial flowing from Article 21 is available to accused at all stages namely the stage of investigation, inquiry, trial, appeal, revision and retrial.

ADM, Jabalpur v. Shivkant Shukla[AIR 1976 SC 1207]

The detenue challenged Sec. 16-A of the MISA (now repealed). The detention was challenged as being violative of Art. 21. The Court held that Article 21 is the sole repository of the right to life and personal liberty and if the right to move to any court for the enforcement of that right was suspended by the Presidential Order under Article 359 the detenue had no locus standi to file a writ petition for challenging the validity of their detention.

Sunil Batra v. Delhi Administration[AIR 1978 SC 1575]

It was held that custodial violence to the arrested person is a grave violation of person's right to life.

Rudal shah v. State of Bihar[AIR 1983 SC 1086]

Supreme Court held that the Court has power to award monetary compensation in appropriate cases where there has been a violation of the Constitutional rights of the citizens. In this case, the SC directed the Bihar Government to pay compensation of Rs. 30,000/- to Rudal Shah who had to remain in the jail for 14 years because of the irresponsible behaviour of the State Govt. Officers even after his acquittal.

Bhim Singh v. State of J & K[(1985) 4 SCC 677]

The Court awarded a compensation of Rs.50,000/- to the petitioner as compensation for the violation of his right to personal liberty. The petitioner, an MLA, was arrested and detained in police custody and deliberately prevented from attending the sessions of the Legislative Assembly.

Bodhisathwa Gautam v. Subhra Chakravorthy[(1996) 1 SCC 490]

Interim compensation to a rape victim was awarded considering his right to life.

M.H. Hoskot v. State of Maharashtra[AIR 1978 SC 1548]

The right to legal aid is one of the ingredients of fair procedure. If a prisoner sentenced to imprisonment, is virtually unable to exercise his constitutional and statutory right of appeal, for want of legal assistance, there is implicit in the court under article 142 read with article 21 and 39-A of the Constitution, power to assign council for such imprisoned individual for doing complete justice. Where the prisoner is disabled from engaging a lawyer, on reasonable grounds such as indigence or incommunicado situation, the court shall, if the circumstances of the case, the gravity of the sentence, and the ends of justice so required, assign competent counsel for the prisoners defence, provided the party doesn't object to that lawyer.

Prem Shankar Shukla v. Delhi Administration[AIR 1980 SC 1535]

The petitioner was an under-trial prisoner in Tihar jail. He was required to be taken from jail to magistrate court and back periodically in connection with certain cases pending against him. The trial court has directed the concerned officer that while escorting him to the court and back, handcuffing should not be done unless it was so warranted. But handcuffing was forced on him by the escorts. He therefore sent a telegram to one of the judges of Supreme Court on the basis of which the present habeas corpus petition has been admitted by the court. To handcuff is to hoop harshly and to punish humiliatingly. The minimum freedom of movement, under which a detainee is entitled to under Art.19, cannot be cut down by the application of handcuffs. Handcuffs must be the last refuge as there are other ways for ensuring security.

Saheli v. Commissioner of Police[AIR 1990 SC 513]

In this case, a 9 year old boy died after being beaten by the Indian Police. The Court directed a payment of Rs 75,000 to the mother of the deceased child and permitted the Delhi Administration to take appropriate steps for the recovery of the amount paid as compensation or part thereof from the officers responsible for this dastardly act. The ambit of right to life has thus widened with the changing times. Many corollary and incidental rights have now been considered to fall under Art.21 and these are now to be ensured as fundamental rights. In a nutshell, various rights involved under article 21 may be enumerated as-

RIGHT TO EDUCATION (Article 21-A)

Article 21-A reads as: -
"The State shall provide free and compulsory education to all children of the age of six to fourteen years in such manner as the State may, by law, determine."

Article 21-A added by the **Constitution (86th Amendment) Act, 2002** makes the education from 6 to 14 years old, a fundamental right, within the meaning of Part III of the Constitution.

Article 21-A may be read with the new substituted **Article 45**and new **clause(k) inserted in Article51-A**by the Constitution (86th Amendment) Act, 2002. To study the status of right to education, it is necessary to understand the relationship between Art.21-A, Art.45 and Art. 51-A (k)

Article 45 calls upon the State *"to endeavour to provide early childhood care and education for all children until they complete the age of six years"*

Clause (k)inserted in **Article 51-A**imposes a fundamental duty on parent/ guardian *"to provide opportunities for education to his child or, as the case may be, ward, between the age of six and fourteen years."*

Mohini Jain V. State of Karnataka[AIR 1992 SC 1858]
(Also known as "Capitation Fee case")

Supreme Court held that right to education is a fundamental right under Art. 21 of the Constitution which cannot be denied by charging a higher fee in the name of 'Capitation fees'.

Facts: In this case, the petitioner Mohini Jain of Meerut, U.P. had challenged the validity of a Notification issued by the government under the Karnataka Educational Institutions (Prohibition of Capitation Fee) Act, 1984 which was passed to regulate tuition fees to be charged by private Medical colleges in the State.

The Notification provided for the following tuition to be charged at the time of admissions-

Candidates on Govt seats – Rs.2,000/- per annum. Karnataka students – Rs.25,000/- per annum.

Students from outside Karnataka – Rs.60,000/-

The petitioner was denied admission on the ground that she was unable to pay such higher tuition fee. The SC held that such a notification is violative of Art.14 and it's arbitrary, unfair and unjust. "The right to education flows directly from the right to life," and the right to education being concomitant to the fundamental right, "The state is under a Constitutional mandate to provide educational institutions at all levels for the benefit of the citizens."

Unni Krishnan v. State of Andhra Pradesh[(1993) 1 SCC 645]

In this case, SC examined the correctness of the Mohini Jain's case judgment. The SC rejected the view held in Mohini Jain's case and held that State is bound only till the age of 14 years to provide free education and the private colleges are no ways bound to provide free education. But, they should be allowed to run their institutions under strict regulatory controls in order to prevent education sector being commercialised. The majority view was that in all such institutions, 50% seats should be filled on merit basis and rest 50% seats may be filled by charging a higher fee.

TMA Pai Foundation v. State of Karnataka[AIR 2003 SC 355]

The scheme as laid down by Unni Krishnan case was rejected and it was held that the private institutions may charge a capitation fee but that always remains in the strict regulation of the State Govt.

DEATH SENTENCE

Various issues involved are- 1.DELAY IN EXECUTION

In *T.V. Vatheeswaram v. State of Tamil Nadu* [AIR 1981 SC 643], the Supreme Court held that delay in execution of death sentence exceeding 2 years would be sufficient ground to invoke protection under Article 21 and the death sentence would be commuted to life imprisonment.

In *Sher Singh v. State of Punjab*[AIR 1983 SC 465], the Supreme Court said that prolonged wait for execution of a sentence of death is an unjust, unfair and unreasonable procedure and the only way to undo that is through Article 21. But the Court held that this cannot be taken as the rule of law and applied to each case and each case should be decided upon its own faces.

2. VALIDITY OF HANGING BY ROPE

The Rajasthan High Court, by an order directed the execution of the death sentence of an accused by hanging at the Stadium Ground of Jaipur. It was also directed that the execution should be done after giving widespread publicity through the media. On receipt of the above order, the Supreme Court in *Attorney General v. Lachma Devi*[AIR 1986 SC 467], held that the said direction for execution of the death sentence was unconstitutional and violative of Article 21. It was further made clear that death by public hanging would be a barbaric practice. Although the crime for which the accused has been found guilty was barbaric it would be a shame on the civilised society to reciprocate the same. The Court said "a barbaric crime should not have to be visited with a barbaric penalty."

RIGHT TO DIE WHETHER COVERED UNDER RIGHT TO LIFE??

This question came for consideration for first time before the High Court of Bombay in ***Stateof Maharashtra v. Maruti Sripati Dubal***[1987 Cr.L.J. 549]

In this case the Bombay High Court held that the right to life guaranteed under Article 21 includes right to die, and the Hon'ble High Court struck down section 309, IPC which provides punishment for attempt to commit suicide by a person as unconstitutional.

In ***P. Rathinam v. Union of India***[(1994) 3 SCC 394] a Division Bench of the Supreme Court supporting the decision of the High Court of Bombay in *Maruti Sripati Dubal Case* held that under Article 21, right to life also include right to die and laid down that Section 309 of Indian Penal Court which deals with attempt to commit suicide is a penal offence and is unconstitutional as well.

This issue again raised before the court in ***Gian Kaur v. State of Punjab***[(1996)2 SCC 648]. In this case a five judge Constitutional Bench of the Supreme Court overruled the P. Ratinam's case and held that "Right to Life" under Article 21 of the Constitution ***does not include "Right to die"***or "Right to be killed" and there is no ground to hold that the section 309, IPC is constitutionally invalid. The true meaning of the word 'life' in Article 21 means life with human dignity. Any aspect of life which makes life dignified may be included in it but not that which extinguishes it. The 'Right to Die' if any, is inherently inconsistent with the "Right to Life" as is "death" with "Life"

A question may arise, in case of a dying man, who is, seriously ill or has been suffering from virulent and incurable form of disease he may be permitted to terminate it by a premature extinction of his life in those circumstances. This category of cases may fall within the ambit of 'Right to Die' with dignity as a part of life with dignity. According to the court these are not cases of extinguishing life but only of accelerating the process of natural death which has already commenced.

EUTHANASIA

Aruna Ramchandra Shanbaug v. Union of India(2011)

On 7 March 2011, the Supreme Court of India legalised passive euthanasia by means of the withdrawal of life support to patients in a permanent vegetative state. The decision was made as part of the verdict in a case involving Aruna Shanbaug, who has been in a vegetative state for 37 years at King Edward Memorial Hospital. The Court rejected active euthanasia by means of lethal injection. In the absence of a law regulating euthanasia in India, the court stated that its decision becomes the law of the land until the Indian parliament enacts a suitable law. Active euthanasia, including the administration of lethal compounds for the purpose of ending life, is still illegal in India, and in most countries. While rejecting Pinki Virani's plea for Aruna Shanbaug's euthanasia, the court laid out guidelines for passive euthanasia. According to these guidelines, passive euthanasia involves the withdrawing of treatment or food that would allow the patient to live. As India had no law about euthanasia, the Supreme Court's guidelines are law until and unless Parliament passes legislation.

The following guidelines were laid down:-

A decision has to be taken to discontinue life support either by the parents or the spouse or other close relatives, or in the absence of any of them, such a decision can be taken even by a person or a body of persons acting as a next friend. It can also be taken by the doctors attending the patient. However, the decision should be taken bona fide in the best interest of the patient.

The question remained as to who is to decide what is the patient's best interest where he is in a ***persistent vegetative state*** (PVS)? Most decisions have held that the decision of the parents, spouse, or other close relative, should carry weight if it is an informed one, but it is not decisive. It is ultimately for the Court to decide, as parens patriae, as to what is in the best interest of the patient, though the wishes of close relatives and next friend, and opinion of medical practitioners should be given due weight in coming to its decision.

Even if a decision is taken by the near relatives or doctors or next friend to withdraw life support, such a decision requires approval from the High Court concerned.

When such an application is filed the Chief Justice of the High Court should forthwith constitute a Bench of at least two Judges who should decide to grant approval or not. A committee of three reputed doctors to be nominated by the Bench, who will give report regarding the condition of the patient. Before giving the verdict a notice regarding the report should be given to the close relatives and the State. After hearing the parties, the High Court can give its verdict.

SAFEGUARDS AGAINST ARBITRARYARREST AND DETENTION[Article 22]

Article 22 of the Constitution provides preventive detention laws. The object of preventive detention is to prevent a person from committing a crime and not to punish him as is done under punitive detention.

*__Article 22__*provides specific rights to arrested and detained persons, in particular the rights to be informed of the grounds of arrest, consult a lawyer of one's own choice, be produced before a magistrate within 24 hours of the arrest, and the freedom not to be detained beyond that period without an order of the magistrate.

The Constitution also authorises the State to make laws providing for preventive detention, subject to certain other safeguards present in Article 22. *__Article 22 Clause (4) to (7) provides for therights of a person detained under preventive detention.__*Art. 22 provides that when a person is detained under any law of preventive detention, the State can detain such person without trial for only three months, and any detention for a longer period must be authorised by an Advisory Board. The person being detained also has the right to be informed about the grounds of detention, and be permitted to make a representation against it, at the earliest opportunity.

Preventive detention has not been unknown in other democratic countries like England and Canada but their recourse has been had to it only in war time. In *__A.K. Gopalan v. State of Madras,__*[AIR 1950 S.C. 27], the Supreme Court had expressed the view that a detenue could not claim the freedom guaranteed by Article 19(l)(d) if it was infringed by his detention.

But this view of the court changed in *__R.C. Cooper v. Union of India,__*[AIR 1970 S.C. 564], and in Maneka Gandhi's case. The court expressed the view in these cases that a law relating to preventive detention must satisfy not only the requirements of Article 22 but also the requirements of Article 21 of the Constitution.

The legislative capacity of Parliament or the State legislatures to enact a law of preventive detention is however, limited to Clauses (4) to (7) of Article 22 which lay down a few safeguards for a person subjected to such detention. The scheme of these clauses is to classify preventive detention in three categories, viz.:

a. *__A preventive detention up to two months, provision for which may be made either by Parliament or a State legislature, in such a case, no reference may be made to an Advisory Board;__*

However, Constitution (44th Amendment Act, 1978) has substituted a new clause for clause

(4) which now reduces the maximum period for which a person may be detained without obtaining the opinion of Advisory Board from 3 months to 2 months. The detention of a person for a longer period than 2 months can only be made after obtaining the opinion of the Advisory Board.

b. ***Preventive detention for over three months subject to safeguard of an Advisory Board consisting of persons qualified to act as High Court judges. No person can remain in preventive detention for more than 3 months unless the Board holds that in its opinion, there are sufficient causes for detention.***

c. ***Preventive detention for over three months without the safeguard of an Advisory Board. Such detention is possible if Parliament prescribes by law the circumstances under which, and the class or classes of cases in which a person may be detained for over three months without reference to Advisory Board.***

Parliament may also prescribe the maximum period for which a person can be detained in cases (b) and (c). This provision, it has been held is merely permissive and does not oblige Parliament to prescribe any maximum period. Further, Parliament may by law prescribe the procedure to be followed by an Advisory Board in an inquiry under Clause (4).

The following safeguards have been provided to a detenue:

1. ***Grounds of detention must be communicated***

Article 22(5)gives the right to the detenue to be communicated the grounds of detention as soon as possible, the detaining authority making the order of detention must as soon as possible communicate to the person detained the grounds of his arrest and to give the detenue the earliest opportunity of making representation against the order of the detention.

The clause (5) of Article 22 imposes an obligation on the detaining authority to furnish to the detenue the grounds for detention, "as soon as possible". The grounds of detention must be clear and easily understandable by the detenue.

2. ***Right of representation***

Article 22imposes an obligation upon the Government to afford the detenue the opportunity to make representation under clause (5) of Article 22. It makes no distinction between order of detention for only two months and less and for those for a longer duration.

The obligation applies to both kinds of orders. It is clear from clauses (4) and (5) of Article 22 that there is dual obligation on the appropriate Government and dual right in favour of detenue, namely, (1) to have his representation irrespective of the length of detention considered by the appropriate Government, and (ii) to have once again in the light of the circumstances of the case considered by Board before it gives its opinion. If in the light of the representation, the Board finds that there is no sufficient cause for detention, the Government has to revoke the order of detention and set at liberty the detenue.

3. *Advisory Board*

Article 22provides that the detenue under the preventive detention law shall have the right to have his representation against his detention reviewed by an Advisory Board. If the Advisory Board reports that the detention is not justified, the detenue must be released forthwith. If the Advisory Board reports that the detention is justified, the government may fix the period for detention.

The Advisory Board must conclude its proceedings expeditiously and must express its opinion within the time prescribed by law. Failure to do that makes detention invalid. Along with its opinion, the Board must forward the entire record to the Government who is supposed to take a decision on the perusal of the entire record.

The Constitution (44th Amendment Act, 1978) has amended Article 22 and reduced the maximum period for which a person may be detained without obtaining the opinion of the Advisory Board from 3 months to 2 months.

It has also changed the constitution of the Board which shall now consist of a Chairman and two other members. The Chairman must be a sitting judge of the appropriate High Court and other members shall be either a sitting or retired judge of a High Court.

The detenue has no right of legal assistance in the proceedings before the Advisory Board. But if the Government is given a facility, it should equally be provided to the detenue.

ADM, Jabalpur v. Shivkant Shukla[AIR 1976 SC 1207]

• 74 •

XI
RIGHT AGAINST EXPLOITATION

RIGHT AGAINST EXPLOITATION[ARTICLES 23 to 24]

The right against exploitation, contained in **_Articles 23–24_**, lays down certain provisions to prevent exploitation of the weaker sections of the society by individuals or the State.

Article 23 provides prohibits human trafficking, making it an offence punishable by law, and also prohibits forced labour or any act of compelling a person to work without wages where he was legally entitled not to work or to receive remuneration for it. However, it permits the State to impose compulsory service for public purposes, including conscription and community service.

The **_Bonded Labour system (Abolition) Act, 1976_**, has been enacted by Parliament to give effect to this Article. Article 24 prohibits the employment of children below the age of 14 years in factories, mines and other hazardous jobs. Parliament has enacted the Child Labour (Prohibition and Regulation) Act, 1986, providing regulations for the abolition of, and penalties for employing, child labour, as well as provisions for rehabilitation of former child labourers.

As per the provisions enshrined the Constitution, the government passed **_"The Immoral Traffic(Prevention) Act 1956"_** and **_"The Bonded Labour System (Abolition) Act 1976."_**

1. Even when the state takes up relief works such as famine or flood relief, it cannot pay less than minimum wages.
2. When the prisoners are sent for the rigorous imprisonment, they must be paid reasonable wages. Please note that as per Supreme Court if a prisoner is not paid wages, it is not a violation of Article

    1. But if the under trials, persons sentences to simple imprisonments and those who have been detained under preventive detention cannot be asked to do manual work. They can do work if they wish to do out of their choice and it would require equitable wages.

What is Bonded Labor?

Bonded Labour or Forced Labour is forbidden. The Forced Labour means not only the physical and legal force *but also arising out of the compulsion of the economic circumstances.*

In this context, the Supreme Court of India in ***People's Union for Democratic Rights andothers v. Union of India and others [1982]***also known as "***Asiad Workers Case***" gave the following explanation:

"We are, therefore, of the view that when a person provides labour of service to another for remuneration which is less than the minimum wage, the labour or service provided by him clearly falls within the scope and ambit of the words "forced labour" under Article 23 of the Constitution of India."

XII
RIGHT TO FREEDOM OF RELIGION

RIGHT TOFREEDOM OF RELIGION[ARTICLES 25 to 28]

The concept of secularism is implicit in the preamble of the Indian Constitution which declares to secure to all its citizens "liberty of thought, expression, belief, faith and worship."The word 'secularism' has been inserted by the *42nd Amendment Act, 1976*. In **_S.R. Bommai v. UoI (1994)_**, the SC has held that "secularism is a basic feature of the Constitution."

The chief aspects of Indian Secularism are:-

1. No State Religion - Separation of State and Religion,
2. Peaceful co-existence of all religions,
3. Treatment of all religions equally by the State,
4. Equality of opportunity in the public field for all, irrespective of caste or creed or race or religion ensuring equal citizenship,
5. Freedom of religion both individual and corporate

The Right to Freedom of Religion, covered in **_Articles 25–28_**, provides religious freedom to all citizens and ensures a secular state in India. According to the Constitution, there is no official State religion, and the State is required to treat all religions impartially and neutrally.

_Article 25_guarantees all persons the freedom of conscience and the right to preach practice and propagate any religion of their choice. This right is, however, subject to public order, morality and health, and the power of the

State to take measures for social welfare and reform. The right to propagate, however, does not include the right to convert another individual, since it would amount to an infringement of the other's right to freedom of conscience.

Article 26guarantees all religious denominations and sects, ***<u>subject to public order, morality</u>***<u>*and health*</u>, *to manage their own affairs in matters of religion, set up institutions of their own for charitable or religious purposes, and own, acquire and manage property in accordance with law*. These provisions do not derogate from the State's power to acquire property belonging to a religious denomination. The State is also empowered to regulate any economic, political or other secular activity associated with religious practice.

Article 27guarantees that no person can be compelled to pay taxes for the promotion of any particular religion or religious institution.

Article 28prohibits religious instruction in a wholly State-funded educational institution, and educational institutions receiving aid from the State cannot compel any of their members to receive religious instruction or attend religious worship without their (or their guardian's) consent.

<u>RESTRICTIONS ON FREEDOM OF RELIGION</u>

1. ***<u>Religious liberty subjected to public order, morality and health</u>*** In the name of religion, no act can be done against public order, morality and health of public. Thus Section 34 of the Police Act prohibits the slaughter of cattle or indecent exposure of one's person in public place. These acts cannot be justified on plea of practice of religious rites. Likewise, in the name of religion 'untouchability' or traffic in human beings' e.g. system of *Dev-dasis* cannot be tolerated. These rights are subjected to the reasonable restrictions under clause (2) of Article

19. For instance, a citizen's freedom of speech and expression in matters of religion is subjected to reasonable restrictions under Article 19 (2). Right to propagate one's religion does not give right to anyone to "forcibly" convert any person to one's own religion. Forcible conversion of any person to one's own religion might disturb the public order and hence could be prohibited by law.

1. ***<u>Regulation of economic, financial, political and secular activities associated with religious</u>***<u>*practices- Clause (2)(a)*</u> - The freedom to practice extends

only to those activities which are the essence of religion. It would not cover secular activities which do not form the essence of religion. It is not always easy to say which activities fall under religious practice or which are of secular, commercial or political nature associated with religion practice. Each case must be judge by its own facts and circumstances.

2. ***Social Welfare and Social Reforms- Clause (2)(b)*** - Under this clause, the State is empowered to make laws for social welfare and social reform. Thus under this clause the State can eradicate social practices and dogmas which stand in the path of the country's onward progress. Such laws do not affect the essence of any religion. Prohibition of evil practices such as *Sati* or system of *Devadasi* has been held to be justified under this clause. The right protected under this clause is a right to enter into a temple for the purpose of worship. But it does not follow from this that, that right is, absolute and unlimited in character. No one can claim that a temple must be kept open for worship at all hours of the day and night or that he should be permitted to perform services personally which the Acharya alone could perform. The State cannot regulate the manner in which the worship of the deity is performed by the authorised *pujaris* of the temple or the hours and days on which the temple is to be kept open for *Darshan* or *Puja* for devotees. The right of Sikhs to wear and carry *Kripan* is recognised as a religious practice in Explanation 1 of Article 25. It does not mean that he can keep any number of *Kripans*. He cannot possess more than one *Kripan* without licence.

FREEDOM TO MANAGE RELIGIOUS AFFAIRS (ARTICLE 26)

Article 26 says that, subject to public order, morality and health, every religious denomination or any section of it shall have the following rights-

a. *to establish and maintain institutions for religious and charitable purpose,*
b. *to manage its own affairs in matters of religion,*
c. *to own and acquire movable and immovable property,*
d. *to administer such property in accordance with law.*

The right guaranteed by Article 25 is an individual right while the right guaranteed by Article 26 is the right of an 'organised body' like the religious denomination or any section thereof.

FREEDOM FROM TAXES FOR PROMOTIONOF ANY PARTICULAR RELIGION (ARTICLE 27)

Article 27provides that no person shall be compelled to pay tax for the promotion or maintenance of any religion or religious denomination. This Article emphasises the secular character of the State. The public money collected by way of tax cannot be spent by the State for the promotion of any particular religion.

PROHIBITION OF RELIGIOUS INSTITUTIONIN STATE AIDED INSTITUTION (ARTICLE 28)

According to ***Article 28(1),***no religious instruction shall be imparted in any educational institution wholly maintained out of State funds. But this clause shall not apply to an educational institution which is administered by the State but was not established under any endowment or trust which requires that religious instruction shall be imparted in such institution. Thus Article 28 mentions four types of educational institutions:

a. ***Institutions wholly maintained by the State.***
b. ***Institutions recognised by the State.***
c. ***Institutions that are receiving aid out of the State fund.***
d. ***Institutions that are administered by the State but are established any trust or endowment.***

In the institutions of (a) type, no religious instructions can be imparted.

In (b) and (c) type of institutions, religious instructions may be imparted only with the consent of the individuals.

In the (d) type institution, there is not restriction on religious instructions.

N Aditya v. Travancore Dewaswom Board

SC held that Brahmins do not have a monopoly over performing puja in a temple and said that a non-brahmin can be appointed as a pujari if he is properly trained and well versed with rituals and the mantras, as necessary to be recited for the particular deity.

Gulam Kadar Ahmadbhai Menon v. Surat Municipal Corporation (1998)

The Gujarat HC held that the right to religion guaranteed to citizens under Art.25 and 26 does not prohibit State to acquire any place of worship for public purpose or a welfare purpose.

Moulana Mufti Sayeed v. State of West Bengal (1999)

The Calcutta HC held that restrictions imposed by the State on the use of microphones and loud-speakers at the time of Azaan are not violative of Art. 25. Azaan is certainly an essential and integral part. Traditionally and according to the religious order, azaan has to be given by the imam or the person-in-charge of the mosques through their own voice and this is sanctioned under the religious order.

Church of God in India v. K.K.R.M.C. Welfare Association (2000)

The SC has held that in the exercise of the right to religious freedom under Articles 25 and 26, no person can be allowed to create noise pollution or disturb the peace of others.

Mohd. Hanif Qureshi v. State of Bihar (1958)

The petitioner claimed that the sacrifice of cows on the occassion of Bakrid was an essential part of his religion and therefore the State law forbidding the slaughter of cows was violative of his right to practise religion. The Court rejected this argument and held that this is not an essential part of the religion and the State can prohibit the same under Art.25 (2).

Rev Stainislaus v. State of M.P.(1958) - Forcible conversion is not allowed in the name of propagation of religion.

Aruna Roy v. Union of India (2002)

The validity of *National Curriculum Framework for School Education, 2000* which provided for education for value development based upon all religions and also a comparative study of philosophy of all religions was challenged on the ground that it was violative of Art.28. Three judge bench of the SC held that the above-said policy was neither violative of Art.28 nor it is against the concept of secularism.

XIII
CULTURAL & EDUCATIONAL RIGHT

<u>CULTURAL & EDUCATIONAL RIGHT [ARTICLES 29 TO 30]</u>

India, being a diverse country with a myriad of ethnic backgrounds, religious influence and varied sub- cultures, also have minority groups. ***<u>Articles 29 to 30</u>***of the Indian Constitution effectively aim to eradicate this problem by making a provision in the article known as 'Right to Cultural and Educational rights of Minority groups'.

The Cultural and Educational rights are measures to protect the rights of cultural, linguistic and religious minorities, by enabling them to conserve their heritage and protecting them against discrimination.

<u>Article 29</u>grants any section of citizens having a distinct language, script culture of its own the right to conserve and develop the same, and thus safeguards the rights of minorities by preventing the State from imposing any external culture on them. It also prohibits discrimination against any citizen for admission into any educational institutions maintained or aided by the State, on the grounds only of religion, race, caste, language or any of them.

However, this is subject to reservation of a reasonable number of seats by the State for socially and educationally backward classes, as well as reservation of up to 50 percent of seats in any educational institution run by a minority community for citizens belonging to that community.

<u>Article 30</u>confers upon all religious and linguistic minorities the right to set up and administer educational institutions of their choice in order to preserve and develop their own culture, and prohibits the State, while granting aid, from discriminating against any institution on the basis of the fact that it is administered by a religious or cultural minority.

The term "**minority**", while not defined in the Constitution, has been interpreted by the Supreme Court to mean any community which numerically forms less than 50% of the population of the state in which it seeks to avail the right under Article 30. In order to claim the right, it is essential that the educational institution must have been established as well as administered by a religious or linguistic minority. Further, the right under Article 30 can be availed of even if the educational institution established does not confine itself to the teaching of the religion or language of the minority concerned, or a majority of students in that institution do not belong to such minority. This right is subject to the power of the State to impose reasonable regulations regarding educational standards, conditions of service of employees, fee structure, and the utilisation of any aid granted by it.

RIGHT TO PROTECTION OF INTERESTS
(ARTICLE 29)

The constitution of India ensures equal to all the citizens of India liberty pertaining to conserving their culture, language and script under **Article 29 (1)**.

This provision simply states that the citizens have the right to preserve their language, heritage and backgrounds and cannot be stifled by major language groups.

The second right under **Article 29 (2)**, says that 'no minority groups will be denied admission into any educational system or institution of their choice, and will also not be deprived of any funds from the state purely based on religion, caste or language'.

In this case, no minority or majority can be denied admission into any state or private institution on the basis of social factors such as language and religion. The institutions have the responsibility of accepting students on the basis of merit and talent, and not on the basis of language, class and religion. The institutions also have to make sure that the cultural diversity of the country is well-maintained in the form of multifarious languages and various religious groups.

Although there appears to be overlapping of provisions in respect to Article 15 (1) and 29 (2), Article 15 (1) is a more general provision stating that there shall be no discrimination on the basis of sex, caste and religion. Article 29, however, is more specific pertaining to a particular species of the system in the form of gaining admission into educational systems and getting benefits from state funds like all other citizens.

RIGHT TO ESTABLISH EDUCATIONAL INSTITUTIONS (ARTICLE 30)

Article 30*of the Indian Constitution states that religious and language minorities will have the right to administer and start their own educational institutions. However, no minority, other than the ones suggested in the article will have the right to establish any institution.*

Article 30 (1A)*- In making any law providing for the compulsory acquisition of any property of an educational institution established and administered by a minority, referred to in clause (1), the State shall ensure that the amount fixed by or determined under such law for the acquisition of such property is such as would not restrict or abrogate the right guaranteed under that clause.*

The second provision, under Article 30 (2) states that, the government will not deny these institutions any state funds or aid on the basis that it is run and managed by minority groups.

PROTECTION OF MINORITY GROUPS

The government has come with varied laws to help protect the rights of the minorities. The Protection of Civil Rights Act 1989 and the Prevention of Atrocities Act of 1989 are two such acts established by the government. The National Commission for Minority Educational Institutions, 1992 was set up to look into any grievances lodged by the minorities or any violation of rights. The commission was also set up to advice the state or central government on any matter relating to the protection of educational minority groups by providing reports and suggestions.

LANDMARK JUDGMENTS ON RIGHT TO ESTABLISH AND ADMINISTER

S.P. Mittal v. UoI (1983)

Validity of **Auroville (Emergency Provisions) Act, 1980** was challenged on the ground of being violative of Art. 29 and 30.

Facts: The society was established to preach and propagate the ideals and teaching of Sri Aurobindo. On receiving complaints about mismanagement of the affairs of the society, the Central Government enacted the Auroville (Emergency Provisions) Act, 1980 for taking over the management of the society. It was held that the Act was not violative of Art. 30. Since the said Society was not a religious denomination, the taking over of the management by the State did not violate Articles 29 and 30 of the Constitution.

State of Madras v. Champakam Dorairajan (1951)

An order of Madras Govt. which fixed the proportion of students of each community that could be admitted into the State Medical and Engineering Colleges. The order was challenged on the ground that it denied admission to a person only on the ground of religion or caste. The petitioners in this case were denied admission only because they were Brahmins. The SC held the order invalid for being violative of Art. 29(2)

State of Bombay v. Bombay Educational Society (1954)

The SC struck down an order of the Bombay Govt. banning admission of those whose language was not English into schools having English as medium of instruction because it denied admission solely on the ground of language.

St. Xaviers College v. State of Gujarat (1974)

The petitioners, a Jesuit Society of Ahmedabad, were running St. Xaviers College of Arts and Commerce in Ahmedabad, which was affiliated to Gujarat University, with the object of giving higher education to the Christian students. The said petitioners challenged certain provisions of the Gujarat University Act, 1949 as being violative of Art. 30. The Court held that the said provisions violated the rights provided by Art.30 and thus does not apply upon the minority institutions.

RIGHT OF A RECOGNITION OR AFFILIATION - NOT A FUNDAMENTAL RIGHT

Affiliation and recognition are matters of policy and the institution seeking recognition or an affiliation has to comply with the basic norms and requirements for claiming the same.

In ***TMA Pai Foundation Judgment***, the Supreme Court has laid down that the right to establish educational institutions of their choice is available not only to the minorities but to all the citizens of the India. One of the fundamental rights in Article 19(1)(g) of the Constitution i.e. **"to practice any profession, or to carry on any occupations, trade or business"** - has been interpreted by the Supreme Court to include right to establish educational institutions, which is a right guaranteed to all the citizens.

What are the actual rights of the minorities?

Minorities can not only establish educational institutions of their choice but also administer them. Supreme Court has further laid down that the right to establish and administer broadly comprises of right to-

a. admit students;

b. set up a reasonable fee structure;

c. constitute a governing body i.e. Management;

d. appoint staff (teaching and non-teaching); and

e. take action if there is dereliction of duty on the part of any employees.

Status of Non-minority Institutions-

Non-minority (i.e., the Majority) educational institutions are governed by the policies and regulations of the state government or the Central Government in matters of admission, appointment of staff, fixing the fee structure and constitution of governing body, whereas the minority institutions are not.

Except the right to establish and administer educational institutions of their choice, there is no other right that minorities enjoy under the Constitution of India.

XIV
RIGHT TO CONSTITUTIONAL REMEDIES

RIGHT TO CONSTITUTIONAL REMEDIES[ARTICLES 32]

Any provision in any Constitution for Fundamental Rights is meaningless unless there are adequate safeguards to ensure enforcement of such provisions. Enforcement of the fundamental right largely depends upon the degree of independence of the Judiciary and the availability of relevant instruments with the executive authority.

Indian Constitution lays down certain provisions to ensure the enforcement of Fundamental Rights. These are as under:

a. The Fundamental Rights provided in the Indian Constitution are guaranteed against any executive and legislative actions. Any executive or legislative action, which infringes upon the Fundamental Rights of any person or any group of persons, can be declared as void by the Courts under Article 13 of the Constitution.

b. In addition, the Judiciary has the power to issue the prerogative writs. These are the extraordinary remedies provided to the citizens to get their rights enforced against any authority in the State. These writs are - *Habeas corpus, Mandamus, Prohibition, Certiorari and Quo warranto*. Both, High Courts as well as the Supreme Court may issue the writs.

The Fundamental Rights provided to the citizens by the Constitution cannot be suspended by the State, except during the period of emergency, as laid down in Article 359 of the Constitution.

However, Article 32 is referred to as the "Constitutional Remedy" for enforcement of Fundamental Rights. This provision itself has been included in the Fundamental Rights and hence it cannot be denied to any person. Dr. B.R. Ambedkar described Article 32 as the heart and soul of Indian Constitution, without which the Constitution would be reduced to nullity.

By including Article 32 in the Fundamental Rights, the Supreme Court has been made the protector and guarantor of these Rights. An application made under Article 32 of the Constitution before the Supreme Court, cannot be refused on technical grounds. In addition to the prescribed five types of writs, the Supreme Court may pass any other appropriate order. Moreover, only the questions pertaining to the Fundamental Rights can be determined in proceedings against Article 32.

Under Article 32, the Supreme Court may issue a writ against any person or government within the territory of India. Where the infringement of a Fundamental Right has been established, the Supreme Court cannot refuse relief on the ground that the aggrieved person may have remedy before some other court or under the ordinary law. The relief can also not be denied on the ground that the disputed facts have to be investigated or some evidence has to be collected. Even if an aggrieved person has not asked for a particular writ, the Supreme Court, after considering the facts and circumstances, may grant the appropriate writ and may even modify it to suit the exigencies of the case.

WRITS

1. **WRIT OF CERTIORARI**
2. **WRIT OF PROHIBITION**
3. **WRIT OF QUO WARRANTO**
4. **WRIT OF MANDAMUS**
5. **WRIT OF HABEAS CORPUS**

Normally, only the aggrieved person is allowed to move the Court. But it has been held by the Supreme Court that in social or public interest matters, any one may move the Court. Any piece of legislation or law, which tends to interfere with the power of Supreme Court under Article 32 shall be declared as void. Hence, there is no way that the legislative or the executive authorities can by-pass the power and responsibility entrusted to the Supreme Court by the Constitution.

1. ***Writ of Habeas corpus***: It is the most valuable **writ for personal liberty**. Habeas Corpus means, "**Let us have the body**." A person, when arrested, can move the Court for the issue of Habeas Corpus. It is an order by a Court to the detaining authority to produce the arrested person before it so that it may examine whether the person has been detained lawfully or otherwise. If the Court is convinced that the person is illegally detained, it can issue orders for his release.

2. ***The Writ of Mandamus***: Mandamus is a Latin word, which means "**We Command**". ***Mandamus is an order from a superior court to a lower court or tribunal or publicauthority to perform an act, which falls within its duty***. It is issued to secure the performance of public duties and to enforce private rights withheld by the public authorities. Simply, it is a writ issued to a public official to do a thing which is a part of his official duty, but, which, he has failed to do, so far. This writ cannot be claimed as a matter of right. It is the discretionary power of a court to issue such writs.

3. ***The Writ of Quo-Warranto***: The word Quo-Warranto literally means "***by what warrants***?" or "***by what authority***". It is a writ issued with a view to restraining a person from acting in a public office to which he is not entitled. The writ of quo warranto is used to prevent illegal assumption of any public office or usurpation of any public office by anybody. For example, a person of 62 years has been appointed to fill a public office whereas the retirement age is 60 years. Now, the appropriate High Court has a right to issue a writ of quo-warranto against the person and declare the office vacant.

4. ***The Writ of Prohibition***: Writ of prohibition means to forbid or to stop and it is popularly known as '***Stay Order***'. This writ is issued when a lower court or a body tries to transgress the limits or powers vested in it. It is a writ issued by a superior court to lower court or a tribunal forbidding it to perform an act outside its jurisdiction. After the issue of this writ, proceedings in the lower court etc. come to a stop.

5. ***The Writ of Certiorari***: Literally, Certiorari means ***to be certified***. The writ of certiorari is ***issued by the Supreme Court to some inferior court or tribunal to transfer the matter to it or to some other superior authority for proper consideration.***

WRITS OF PROHIBITION, MANDAMUS AND CERTIORARI

The writ of prohibition is issued by any High Court or the Supreme Court to any inferior court, prohibiting the latter to continue proceedings in a particular case, where it has no legal jurisdiction of trial. While the writ of mandamus commands doing of particular thing, the writ of prohibition is essentially addressed to a subordinate court commanding inactivity. Writ of prohibition is, thus, not available against a public officer not vested with judicial or quasi-judicial powers. The Supreme Court can issue this writ only where a fundamental right is affected.

The writ of certiorari can be issued by the Supreme Court or any High Court for quashing the order already passed by an inferior court. In other words, *while the prohibition is available at the earlier stage, certiorari is available on similar grounds at a later stage. It can also be said that the writ of prohibition is available during the pendency of proceedings before a sub-ordinate court, certiorari can be resorted to only after the order or decision has been announced.*

There are several conditions necessary for the issue of writ of certiorari, which are as under:

a. There should be court, tribunal or an officer having legal authority to determine the question of deciding fundamental rights with a duty to act judicially.
b. Such a court, tribunal or officer must have passed order acting without jurisdiction or in excess of the judicial authority vested by law in such court, tribunal or law.

The order could also be against the principle of natural justice or it could contain an error of judgment in appreciating the facts of the case.

ಬಂ

XV
DIRECTIVE PRINCIPLE OF STATE POLICY

Introduction-

Part IV of the Constitution of Indian contains Directive Principles of State Policy which extends from ***Articles 36 to 51***(both inclusive). The concept of Directive Principles under Part IV of Indian Constitution have been inspired by the Directive Principles given in the **Constitution of Ireland** and also by the principles of Gandhism; and relate to social justice, economic welfare, foreign policy, and legal and administrative matters.

In previous days, it was thought that the main duty of state is the maintenance of law and order and the protection of life, liberty and property of the subjects. This was rather a restrictive approach towards the concept of State. The Directive Principles are certain active obligations or guidelines to State which lay down certain economic and social goal to be pursued by the State to attain a welfare State. These principles impose certain obligations on the state to take positive action in certain directions in order to promote the welfare of the people and achieve economic democracy. If we go through the 16 articles contained in Part IV, we will find that these directives extend to almost every field of life, i.e., economic, social, legal, environmental.

<u>**EXTENT TO WHICH THE EXECUTIVE, LEGISLATURE ANDJUDICIARY IS OBLIGED TO FOLLOW**</u>

<u>**THE DIRECTIVE PRINCIPLES OF STATE POLICY**</u>

According to **_Article 37_**, the directive principles **shall not be enforceable by any court**, but these principles are fundamental in the governance of the country and it shall be the duty of the state to apply them in making laws.

Here, the word 'State' includes the executive, the legislature and the judiciary. Hence a duty has been imposed upon the organs of the Government to apply these principles in making laws. It is the duty of the Judiciary to interpret the law in the light of these directive principles.

Supreme Court in many decisions has laid down the following two propositions–

i.   The directive principles run as subsidiary to the fundamental rights.
ii. The directive principles can also be taken into consideration in constructing the ambiguous provisions of the Constitution.

CHARACTERISTICS OFDIRECTIVE PRINCIPLES

- They are not enforceable in any law courts and therefore if a directive is not obeyed or implemented by the State, its obedience or implementation cannot be secured through judicial proceedings
- These are fundamental in the governance of the country and it shall be the duty of the State to apply these principles in making laws

VARIOUS PROVISIONS FALLING UNDER PART IV COMPRISING THEDIRECTIVE PRINCIPLES OF STATE POLICY

Despite being non-justiciable, the Directive Principles act as a check on the State; theorized as a yardstick in the hands of the electorate and the opposition to measure the performance of a government at the time of an election.

_Article 37_while stating that the Directive Principles are not enforceable in any court of law, declares them to be "fundamental to the governance of the country" and imposes an obligation on the State to apply them in matters of legislation. Thus, they serve to emphasize the welfare state model of the Constitution and emphasize the positive duty of the State to promote the welfare of the people by affirming social, economic and political justice, as well as to fight income inequality and ensure individual dignity, as mandated by Article 38.

_Article 39_lays down certain principles of policy to be followed by the State, including providing an adequate means of livelihood for all citizens, equal pay for equal work for men and women, proper working conditions, reduction of the concentration of wealth and means of production from the hands of a few, and distribution of community resources to "sub-serve the common good". These clauses highlight the Constitutional objectives of building an egalitarian social order and establishing a welfare state, by bringing about a social revolution assisted by the State, and has been used to support the nationalisation of mineral resources as well as public utilities. Further, several legislations pertaining to agrarian reform and land tenure have been enacted by the federal and state governments, in order to ensure equitable distribution of land resources.

_Article 39A_requires the State to provide free legal aid to ensure that opportunities for securing justice are available to all citizens irrespective of economic or other disabilities.

_Article 40_provides that the State shall take steps to organize village panchayats and endow them with such powers and authority as may be necessary to enable them to function as units of self- government.

Articles 41–43 mandate the State to endeavour to secure to all citizens the right to work, to secure a living wage, ensure social security, render maternity relief, and a decent standard of living. These provisions aim at establishing a socialist state as envisaged in the Preamble.

Article 43 also places upon the State the responsibility of promoting cottage industries, and the federal government has, in furtherance of this, established several Boards for the promotion of khadi, handlooms etc., in coordination with the state governments.

Article 43A mandates the State to work towards securing the participation of workers in the management of industries.

Article 44 encourages the State to secure a uniform civil code for all citizens, by eliminating discrepancies between various personal laws currently in force in the country. However, this has remained a "dead letter" despite numerous reminders from the Supreme Court to implement the provision.

Article 45 originally mandated the State to provide free and compulsory education to children between the ages of six and fourteen years, but after the **_86th Amendment in 2002_**, this has been converted into a Fundamental Right and replaced by an obligation upon the State to secure early childhood care to all children below the age of six.

Article 46 makes it mandatory upon the State to promote the interests of and work for the economic uplift of the scheduled castes and scheduled tribes and protect them from discrimination and exploitation. Several enactments, including two Constitutional amendments i.e., 73rd and 74th Constitutional Amendments, have been passed to give effect to this provision.

_Article 47_commits the State to raise the standard of living and improve public health, and prohibit the consumption of intoxicating drinks and drugs injurious to health. As a consequence, partial or total prohibition has been introduced in several states, but financial constraints have prevented its full-fledged application.

Article 48 makes it mandatory upon the State to organise agriculture and animal husbandry on modern and scientific lines by improving breeds and prohibiting slaughter of cattle.

Article 48A mandates the State to protect the environment and safeguard the forests and wildlife of the country.

Article 49 places an obligation upon the State to ensure the preservation of monuments and objects of national importance.

Article 50 requires the State to ensure the separation of judiciary from executive in public services, in order to ensure judicial independence, and federal legislation has been enacted to achieve this objective.

The State, according to **_Article 51_**, must also strive for the promotion of international peace and security, and Parliament has been empowered under Article 253 to make laws giving effect to international treaties.

CLASSIFICATION OF DIRECTIVE PRINCIPLES OF STATE POLICY

There is a classification of the Directive principles of State policy according to which the Constitutional draftsmen have classified the articles or the provisions falling under Part IV on the basis of their basic purposes or the legislative intent. There are three kinds of Directive Principles of State Policy as enumerated in the Constitution of India from Article 38 to Article 51.

1. **_The directives in the nature of ideals of the State are-_**
2. The State shall strive to promote the welfare of the people by securing a social order permeated by social, economic and political justice (Art. 38).
3. The State shall endeavour to secure just and humane conditions of work a living wage a decent standard of living and social and cultural opportunities for all workers (Art 43).
4. The State shall endeavour to raise the level of nutrition and standard of living and to improve the health of the people (Art. 47).

5. The State shall endeavour to promote international peace and amity (Art. 51)

6. The State shall direct its policy towards securing equitable distribution of the material resources of the community and prevention of concentration of wealth and means of production to the common detriment (Art . 39)

2. *Directives in the nature of policy of the State–*

a. To establish economic democracy and justice by securing certain economic rights.
b. To secure a uniform civil code for the citizen. (Art. 44)
c. To provide free and compulsory primary education (Art. 45)
d. To prohibit consumption of liquor and intoxicating drug except for medical purposes (Art. 47).
e. To develop cottage industries (Art. 43).
f. To organise agriculture and animal husbandry on modern lines (Art. 48).
g. To prevent slaughter of useful cattle i.e., cows, calves and other milch and draught, cattle (Art. 48).
h. To organise village Panchayats as units of self-government (Art. 40),
a. To protect and improve the environment and to safeguards forest and wild life (Art. 48A).
j. To protect and maintain places of historic or artistic interest (Art. 49).
k. To separate the Judiciary from the Executive (Art. 50).

3. *Directives in the nature of non-justiciable rights of every citizen-*

a. Right to adequate means of livelihood (Art. 39 (a))
b. Right to both sexes to equal pay for equal work (Art. 39 (d))
c. Right against economic exploitation (Art. 39(e), (f)).
d. Right to work (Art.41)
e. Right to education (Art.45).

IMPORTANCE OF DIRECTIVE PRINCIPLES

• The Directive Principles are fundamental in the smooth governance of the States

- The Directive Principles lay down the foundation of economic democracy.
- These are measuring rods to judge the achievements of the Government.
- The Directive Principles aim to establish a welfare state.
- These principles supplement the Fundamental rights.
- These principles also serve as guiding principles for courts.
- They bring stability and continuity in State policies.

WHY DID THE FRAMERS OF THE CONSTITUTION MADEDIRECTIVE PRINCIPLES NON-JUSTICIABLE IN NATURE?

- India as a country didn't possess enough financial resources to implement the directions given in the directive principles.
- Moreover, vast diversity and backwardness in the country posed as a hurdle in the way of their implementation.
- India after independence had many preoccupations i.e., various regions had their unique set of problems which they needed to deal with them on priority. If these directive principles were made compulsory they would have added to the burden on these regions.

CRITICISM OF DIRECTIVE PRINCIPLES OF STATE POLICY

- Although very noble in thought but the Directive Principles are non-justiciable in nature.
- Directive Principles are nothing more than moral principles or obligations.
- Directive Principles are neither properly classified nor logically arranged.
- Some Directive Principles are not practicable.
- Directive Principles are foreign in nature.
- Directive Principles are actually against the principle of State Sovereignty.
- It is illogical to include these principles in the Constitution.
- These are responsible for Constitutional conflicts.
- No mention of methods to implement these has been provided.

DIFFERENCE BETWEEN FUNDAMENTAL RIGHTS AND DIRECTIVE PRINCIPLES OF STATE POLICY

FUNDAMENTAL RIGHTS

- Part III—Arts. 12 to 35 deal with Fundamental Rights
- Fundamental rights mainly aimed at assuring political freedom to the citizen by protecting against State action.
- Fundamental rights are justiciable rights
- Fundamental rights are sacrosanct and not liable to be curtailed by the State action.
- Fundamental rights are negative in character and the State not to do certain things.
- Fundamental rights described by the Supreme Court as transcended 'inalienable' and personal.
- Fundamental rights considered as means by which goals to be achieved.

DIRECTIVE PRINCIPLESOF STATE POLICY

- Part 1V—Arts. 36 to 51 deal with Directive principles.
- Directive principles are aimed at securing social and economic freedom by appropriate State action.
- Directive principles are justiciable rights.
- Directive principles are sacrosanct.
- Directive principles are positive in character and the State is directed to take certain positive steps.
- Directive principles described by the Supreme Court as conscience or the Constitution.
- Directive principles prescribed the goals to be attained.

RELATIONSHIP BETWEEN FUNDAMENTAL RIGHTSAND DIRECTIVE PRINCIPLES OF STATE

Champakam Dorairajan Case (1951)

Supreme Court (SC) in its verdict said that in case of conflict between Fundamental Rights and Directive Principles, Fundamental Rights would always prevail. It also said that Directive principles have to work as a supplement with Fundamental rights & Parliament can't amend Fundamental Rights.

Golaknath Case (1967)

SC held that Parliament cannot amend Fundamental Rights to give effect to the Directive Principles.

24th Amendment Act, 1971

This amendment was done in reaction to Golaknath Case judgement and to nullify the effect of the same. It declared that Parliament has the right to amend the Fundamental Right by use of a Constitutional Amendment. It was also done in reaction to Golaknath Case judgement. It inserted a new Article 31-C which contained the following two provisions:

25th Amendment Act, 1971

i. No law which gives effect to the directive principles can be declared invalid and unconstitutional on the grounds that it is violating fundamental rights namely Article 14 (equality before law and equal protection of laws), Article 19(protection of six rights in respect of speech, assembly, movement, etc.) & Article 31(right to property).

ii. No law containing a declaration for giving effect to such policy shall be questioned in any court on the ground that it does not give effect to such a policy.

Kesavananda Bharti Case (1973)

SC in its verdict held that the second provision mentioned in the Article 31-C is invalid & unconstitutional as it is taking away the power of court for judicial review. However, first provision of Article 31-C was held valid & constitutional.

42nd Amendment Act, 1976

Position of Directive Principles was made superior to Fundamental Rights

Minerva Mills Case (1980)

SC in its decision declared that Directive Principles are subordinate to Fundamental Rights. But position of Fundamental Rights under Article 14 & Article 19 was made subordinate to Directive Principles. SC also said that Constitution demands to maintain balance between the Fundamental Rights & Directive principles. To give absolute primacy to one over the other is to disturb the harmony of the Constitution.

[**Note: Right to property (Article 31) was abolished as a fundamental right by 44th Amendment Act (1978)]**

Present Position

For now, Fundamental Rights enjoy supremacy over Directive Principles **(except Article 14 & Article 19).** Parliament is entitled to amend Fundamental Right in order to give effect to the Directive Principles as long as it does not affect to the basic structure of the Constitution.

XVI
FUNDAMENTAL DUTIES

Rights and Duties are like two sides of a coin, absolutely inseparable. Whenever and wherever we have any rights, we must have corresponding duties. Whether it be the home, the society or the country, in every sphere of life we have rights and duties that go hand in hand. We have rights in the same measure as we have duties. The Fundamental Duties are a novel feature of the Indian Constitution. No democratic polity can ever succeed where the citizens are not willing to be active participants in the process of governance by assuming responsibilities and discharging citizenship duties and coming forward to give their best to the country.

ORIGIN: The Fundamental Duties of citizens were ***added to the Constitution by the 42nd Amendment in 1976 by way of inserting* PART IV-A *upon the recommendations of the* Swaran Singh Committee**that was constituted by the government earlier that year. All the fundamental duties were incorporated in one article only i.e., **_Article 51-A_**. Originally, constitution had only 10 fundamental duties. Originally ten in number, the Fundamental Duties were increased to eleven by the 86th Amendment in 2002, which added a duty on every parent or guardian to ensure that their child or ward was provided opportunities for education between the ages of six and fourteen years. The idea for Fundamental Duties has been borrowed from erstwhile **_USSR_**.

Fundamental duties are obligatory in nature. But there is no provision in the constitution for direct enforcement of these duties. There is no sanction either to prevent their violation. However, the importance of fundamental duties can be gauged from the following facts:

a. As rights and duties are the two side of the same coin, it is expected that one should observe one's duties in order to seek the enforcement of one's fundamental rights, in the context if a person approaches the court for the enforcement of any of his fundamental rights, the court may refuse to take a lenient view of him if it comes to know that the concerned individual has no respect for what is expected of him by the state as a citizen of the country.

a. They can be used for interpreting ambiguous statutes. The court may look at the fundamental duties while interpreting equivocal statutes which admit of two constructions.

c. While determining the constitutionality of any law, if court finds that it seeks to give effect to any of the duties, it may consider such law to be 'reasonable', and thereby, save such law from unconstitutionality.

FUNDAMENTAL DUTIES IN INDIA

Under **Article 51-A** of Indian Constitution, every citizen has been obligated to perform certain duties called the ***Fundamental Duties***. These duties are defined as the ***moral obligations of allcitizens* to help promote a spirit of patriotism and to uphold the unity of India.**

The following are the Eleven Fundamental Duties of every citizen of India:

a. ***To abide by the Constitution and respect the National Flag and the National Anthem;***

The first and the foremost duty assigned to every citizen of India is to abide by the Constitution and respect its ideals and institutions, the National Flag and the National Anthem. These are the very physical foundations of our citizenship. Citizens are supposed to maintain the dignity of the Constitution by not indulging in any activities in violation of the letter or spirit of the Constitution. Ours is a vast country with many languages, sub-cultures and religious and ethnic diversities, but the essential unit of the country is epitomized in the one Constitution, one flag, one people and single citizenship. We are all governed and guided by this Constitution irrespective of caste, religion, race, sex, etc. National Flag and the National Anthem are symbols of our history, sovereignty, unity and pride. We, the citizens of India, have to be equally proud of our nation, our Constitution, our National Flag and our National Anthem. We must put the nation above our narrow personal interests and then only we will be able to protect our hard-earned freedom and sovereignty.

b. *To cherish and follow the noble ideals which inspired our national struggle for freedom;*

The citizens of India must cherish and follow the noble ideals which inspired the national struggle for freedom. The battle of freedom was a long one where thousands of people sacrificed their lives for our freedom. It becomes our duty to remember the sacrifices made by our forefathers for the cause of the country. But what is much more important is to remember, imbibe and follow the ideals which pervaded our unique struggle. It was not a struggle merely for political freedom of India. It was for the social and economic emancipation of the people all over the nation. If we, the citizens of India remain conscious of and committed to these ideals, then only we will be able to do justice with the great struggle of our freedom fighters.

c. *To uphold and protect the sovereignty, unity and integrity of India;*

It imposes a Fundamental Duty on every citizen of India that he shall not do anything derogatory of upholding or protecting the sovereignty, unity or integrity of India. It is a duty prohibitory in nature addressed to traitors and spies.

d. *To defend the country and render national service when called upon to do so;*

In modern nation States, it is goes without saying that every citizen is bound to be ready to defend the country against war or external aggression. The present-day wars are not fought on the battlefield only nor are they won only by the armed forces; the citizens at large play a most vital role in a variety of ways. Sometimes, civilians may be required also to take up arms in defence of the country.

e. ***To promote harmony and the spirit of common brotherhood amongst all people of Indiatranscending religious, linguistic and regional or sectional diversities and to renouncepractices derogatory to the dignity of women;***

The duty to promote harmony and the spirit of common brotherhood amongst all the people of India essentially flows from the basic value of fraternity enshrined in the Preamble to the Constitution. India is a country of different castes, languages, religions and many cultural streams but we are one people with one Constitution, one flag and single citizenship. Spirit of brotherhood should come very normally among the citizens of a country like India where the norm has been to consider the entire world as one family. The Constitution also casts upon us the Fundamental Duty of ensuring that all practices derogatory to the dignity of women are renounced. This again should come normally to a country where it is a saying that Gods reside where women are worshipped.

f. ***To value and preserve the rich heritage of our composite culture;***

Our cultural heritage is one of the noblest and the richest. What we have inherited from the past, we must preserve and pass on to the future generations. In fact, each generation leaves its footprints on the sands of time. We must hold precious and dear what our fore-fathers have created and their successive generations bequeathed to us as symbols of their artistic excellence and achievements. Generations to come will always draw an inspiration from past history which stimulates them to aim at ever greater heights of achievement and excellence. It becomes the ardent duty of every citizen to ensure that these monuments and pieces of art are not in any way damaged, disfigured, scratched or subjected to vandalism or greed of unscrupulous traders and smugglers.

g. ***To protect and improve the natural environment including forests, lakes, rivers and wildlife and to have compassion for living creatures;***

In the face of the menace of the increasing pollution and environmental degradation, it is the duty of every citizen to protect and improve natural environment including forests, lakes, rivers and wild life and to have compassion for living creatures. The rising air, water and noise pollution and large-scale denudation of forest are causing immense harm to all human life on earth. The mindless and wanton deforestation in the name of needs of development is causing havoc in the form of natural calamities and imbalances. By protecting our forests, planting new trees, cleaning rivers, conserving water resources, reforesting wastelands, hills and mountains and controlling pollution in cities, villages and industrial units, we can help save the future of our coming generations and of planet itself. What is needed is a concerted effort at, an awareness campaign and a planned strategy to move forward through voluntary citizen initiatives. Governmental steps alone would not suffice.

h. ***To develop the scientific temper, humanism and the spirit of inquiry and reform;***

It is the bounden duty of every citizen to preserve and promote a scientific temper and a spirit of inquiry to keep pace with the fast-changing world.

i. ***To safeguard public property and to abjure violence;***

It is most unfortunate that in a country which preaches non-violence to the rest of the world, we see from time-to-time instances of senseless violence and destruction of public property indulged in by a few of its citizens. This is why it became necessary to prescribe the responsibility "to safeguard public property and abjure violence" as a fundamental duty of the citizens.

j. ***To strive towards excellence in all spheres of individual and collective activity, so that thenation constantly rises to higher levels of endeavour and achievement;***

The drive for excellence in all spheres of individual and collective activity is the demand of times and a basic requirement in a highly competitive world. This would include respect for professional obligations and excellence.

k. ***To provide opportunities for education by the parent the guardian, to his child, or a wardbetween the age of 6-14 years as the case may be.***

Significant points of Fundamental Duties

- The Fundamental Duties of citizens were added to the Constitution by the 42nd Amendment in 1976, upon the recommendations of the Swarn Singh Committee that was constituted by the government earlier that year.
- Fundamental duties are applicable only to citizens and not to the aliens.
- India borrowed the concept of Fundamental Duties from USSR.
- The inclusion of Fundamental Duties brought our Constitution in line with Article 29 (1) of the Universal Declaration of Human Rights and with provisions in several modern Constitutions of other countries.
- Out of the ten clauses in Article 51A, six are positive duties and the other five are negative duties. Clauses (b), (d), (f), (h), (j) and (k) require the citizens to perform these Fundamental Duties actively.
- It is suggested that a few more Fundamental Duties, namely, duty to vote in an election, duty to pay taxes and duty to resist injustice may be added in due course to Article 51A.
- A number of judicial decisions are available towards the enforcement of certain clauses under Article 51A.
- Comprehensive legislation is needed for clauses (a), (c), (e), (g) and (i). The remaining 5 clauses, which are exhortation of basic human values, have to be developed amongst citizens through the education system by creating proper and graded curricular input from primary level of education to the higher and professional levels.

Some legal provisions in consonance with the Fundamental Duties are-

a. In order to ensure that no disrespect is shown to the National Flag, Constitution of India and the National anthem, the **Prevention of Insults to National Honour Act, 1971** was enacted.

b. The **Emblems and Names (Prevention of Improper Use) Act, 1950** was enacted soon after independence to prevent improper use of the National Flag and the National Anthem.

c. There are a number of provisions in the existing criminal laws to ensure that the activities which encourage enmity between different groups of people on grounds of religion, race, place of birth, residence, language, etc. are adequately punished. Writings, speeches, gestures, activities, exercise, drills, etc. aimed at creating a feeling of insecurity or ill-will among the members of other communities, etc. have been prohibited under **Section 153-A of the Indian Penal Code, 1860.**

d. Imputations and assertions prejudicial to the national integration constitute a punishable offence under **Section 153-B of the Indian Penal Code, 1860.**

e. A Communal organization can be declared unlawful association under the provisions of**Unlawful Activities (Prevention) Act, 1967.**

f. Offences related to religion are covered in **Sections 295-298 of the Indian Penal Code.**

g. Provisions of the **Protection of Civil Rights Act, 1955 (earlier the Untouchability (Offences) Act, 1955).**

h. **Sections 123(3) and 123(3A) of the Representation of People Act, 1951** declares that soliciting of vote on the ground of religion and the promotion or attempt to promote feelings of enmity or hatred between different classes of citizens of India on the grounds of religion, race, caste, community or language is a corrupt practice. A person indulging in a corrupt practice can be disqualified for being a Member of Parliament or a State Legislature under **Section 8A of the Representation of People Act, 1951.**

- ***Bijoe Emannuel v. State of Kerala [AIR 1987 SC 758]****-* The Supreme court held that proper respect was shown by the students to the National them by standing up in silence when the National anthem was sung. By not joining in the singing, the Court held, did not amount to committing disrespect to the National Anthem.

XVII
UNION EXECUTIVE

The Union Executive broadly covers the President, Council of Ministers and the Prime Minister. Under the Indian Constitution, the President of India enjoys a unique position. President is the **head of the Union Executive.** *Article 52* creates the position of the President. The **President of India** is the head of state of the Republic of India. He is considered to be above party politics and is **nota member of any political party**.

The President is the **first citizen of the country** and **formal head ofthe executive, legislature and judiciary of India.** He is also the **commander-in-chief of the Indian Armed Forces**. He represents sovereignty of the country. He is elected by the elected representatives of the people.

POSITION OF THE PRESIDENT UNDER INDIAN CONSTITUTION

Article 52 provides that there shall be a President of India and *Article 53* provides that the executive powers of the Union shall be vested in the President of India and shall be exercised either directly or through officers subordinate to him in accordance with the *Constitution*. Thus, President of India is bound to act in accordance with the Constitution.

Also, *Article 74* of the Constitution provides that there shall be Council of Ministers with the Prime Minister at the head to aid and advice the President of India. Thus, a question arises what does aid and advise mean? Can President of India refuse or disallow or disregard the advice tendered or given by the Council of Ministers to the President? As *Article 75 (3)* provides, the Council of Ministers shall be collectively responsible to the House of the People. In Parliamentary form of Government, Council of Ministers is responsible to the Lok Sabha. Similarly, if President does not act in accordance with the Constitution, then there is provision for his impeachment. Under Article 368, a provision has been made that if any Amendment Act has been passed in order to amend the Constitution, the President shall have to sign it. It is very clear from all the above provisions that President cannot go against the wishes of the Council of Ministers as headed by the Prime Minister. He is said to be a puppet in the hands of Prime Minister.

DUTIES OF THE PRESIDENT

The primary duty of the President is to preserve, protect and defend the Constitution and the law of India as made part of his oath (***Article 60***). He is liable for impeachment for violation of the Constitution (***Article 61***).

The Constitution of India envisages a parliamentary Government in India. ***Part V*** of the Constitution of India deals with the office of the President of India. Although Article 53 of the Constitution says that the executive power of union shall be exercised by the President either directly or through officers' sub-ordinate to him.

QUALIFICATIONS TO BE ELECTED A PRESIDENT

In practice the President has to abide by the decisions of the council of ministers with the Prime Ministers at the head. Our Constitution is a harmonious blend of the political systems of the U.S.A. and the U.K. The President merely represents the nation, he does not rule.

The candidate-

a. Should be a citizen of India;
b. Should be of not less than 35 years of age;
c. Should be qualified for elections as a member of the House of people; and
d. Should not hold any office of profit under the Government of India or any state Government or any local authority subject to the control of any of these Government;
e. Must not be a member of the parliament.

ELECTION OF THE PRESIDENT

The founding fathers of the Constitution did not provide for the popular election of the President.

Article 54 of the Indian Constitution provides for the election of the President of India.

The President of India is elected by indirect election that is by an electoral college through secret ballot, in accordance with the system of proportional representation by means of the single transferable vote.

As far as practicable, there shall be uniformity of representation of the different states at the election, according to the population and the total number of elected members of the Legislative Assembly of each state, and party shall also be maintained between the State as a whole and the Union *(Article 55). **Electoral College which elects President consists of-***

- Elected members of both the Houses of Parliament (does not include nominated members)
- Electoral college which elects the President consists of elected MP's and elected MLAs at the state level
- MLAs of National Capital Territory of Delhi and the Union territory of Pondicherry are also included

SINGLE TRANSFERABLE VOTE

The election of the President is held through single transferable vote system of proportional representation. Under this system names of all the candidates are listed on the ballot paper and the elector gives them numbers according to his/her preference. Every voter may mark on the ballot paper as many preferences as there are candidates. Thus, the elector shall place the figure 1 opposite the name of the candidate whom he/she chooses for first preference and may mark as many preferences as he/she wishes by putting the figures 2, 3, 4 and so on against the names of other candidates. The ballot becomes invalid if first preference is marked against more than one candidate or if the first preference is not marked at all.

As far as practicable, there shall be uniformity in the scale of representation of the different States at the election of the President. For the purpose of securing such uniformity among the States 'inter se' as well as parity between the States as a whole and the Union, the number of votes which each elected member of Parliament and of the Legislative Assembly of each State is entitled to cast at such election shall be determined in the following manner-

a. Every elected member of the Legislative Assembly of a State shall have as many votes as there are multiples of one thousand in the quotient obtained by dividing the population of the State by the total number of the elected members of the Assembly;
b. if, after taking the said multiple of one thousand; the remainder is not less than five hundred than the vote of each member referred to in sub-

clause (a) shall be further increased by one;

c. Each elected member of either House of Parliament shall have such number of votes as may be obtained by dividing the total number of votes assigned to the members of the Legislative Assemblies of the States under sub-clause (a) and (b) by the total number of the elected members of both Houses of Parliament, fractions exceeding one-half being counted as one and other fractions disregarded.

The election of the President shall be held in accordance with the ***system of proportional representation by means of the single transferable vote and the voting at such election shall be bythe secret ballot.***In this Article, the expression "population" means the population as ascertained at the preceding census of which the relevant figures have been published. **[Article 55]**

Conditions of President's office - ***Article 59***of the Constitution lays down the conditions-

a. The President cannot be a member of either of House of Parliament or State Legislature when holding the office of President.
b. The President cannot hold any other office of profit.
c. Parliament by law will determine the salary of President.

Term of office: The President's term of office is for ***five years***from the date on which he enters upon his office; but he is eligible for re-election.

The President office may terminate within the term of five years in either of two ways-

a. By resignation in writing under his hand addressed to the vice-President of India,
b. By removal for violation of the constitution, by the process of impeachment (Art. 56).

VACANCY IN THE OFFICE OF PRESIDENT

A vacancy in the office of the President may be caused in way of the following ways-

i. On the expiry of his term of five years,
ii. By his death,

iii. By his resignation. The President may, by writing under his hand addressed to the Vice- President, resign from his office,

iv. On his removal by impeachment,

The President may, for violation of the Constitution, be removed from the office by impeachment in the manner provided in Art. 61

i. Otherwise, e.g., on the setting aside of his election as President.

TIME FOR HOLDING PRESIDENTIAL ELECTIONS

a. An election to fill a vacancy caused by the expiration of the term of office of President shall be completed before the expiration of the current term.

b. An election to fill a vacancy in the office of President occurring by the reasons of death, resignation or removal, or otherwise, should be held within 6 months from the date of occurrence of vacancy.

PRIVILEGES AND IMMUNITIES

a. The President cannot be asked to be present in any court of law during his tenure.

b. A prior notice of two months' time is to be served before instituting a civil case against him.

c. The President can neither be arrested nor any criminal proceedings be instituted against him in any court of law during his tenure.

REMOVAL OF PRESIDENT (IMPEACHMENT PROCESS)

The President can only be removed from office through a process called *impeachment*. The Constitution lays down a detailed procedure for the impeachment of the President. An impeachment is a quasi-judicial procedure in parliament. Either House may prefer the charge of violation of the Constitution before the other House which shall then either investigate the charge itself or cause the charge to be investigated.

PROCEDURE FOR IMPEACHMENT

If the charges are accepted by a two-third majority of the total membership of the second House, the impeachment succeeds. The President thus stands removed from the office from the date on which the resolution is passed.

The charges levelled against the President are investigated by the second House. President has the right to be heard or defended when the charges against him are being investigated. The President may defend himself in person or through

his counsel.

The resolution to impeach the President can be moved in either House of Parliament. ***Such a resolution can be moved only after a notice has been given by***

at least one-fourth of the total number of members of the House.Such a resolution charging the President for violation of the Constitution must be passed by a majority of not less than two-third of the total membership of that House before it goes to the other House for investigation.

The President is not answerable to any court of law for the exercise of his functions.

But the charge cannot be preferred by a House unless-

a. a resolution containing the proposal is moved after a 14 days notice in writing signed by not less than 1/4 of the total number of members of the House; and

b. the resolution is then passed by a majority of not less than 2/3 of the total membership of the House.

The President shall have a right to appear and to be represented at such investigation. If as a result of the investigation, a resolution is passed by not less than 2/3 of the total membership of the House before which the charge has been preferred declaring that the charge has been sustained, such resolution shall have the effect of removing the President from his office with effect from the date on which such resolution is passed ***(Article 61)***.

Since the Constitution provides the mode and ground for removing the President, he cannot be removed otherwise than by impeachment, in accordance with the terms of Art 56 and 61.

ALLOWANCES AND EMOLUMENTS

The President shall be entitled without payment of rent to the use of his official residence and shall be also entitled to such emoluments, allowances and privileges as may be determined by Parliament by law that behalf is so made, such emoluments, allowances and privileges as are specified in the second schedule of the Constitution.

The President receives a salary of **Rs. 1,50,000/- per month** and an annual pension on the expiration of his term or on resignation provided he is not re-elected to the office. The emoluments and allowances of the President shall not be diminished during his term of office.

POWERS OF THE PRESIDENT

The President of India is the head of a parliamentary state, entrusted with all the executive authorities including the supreme command of the forces. He exercises his power with the aid and advice of the Council of Ministers.

The Prime Minister is the real head of the Government. However, a vast number of powers have been earmarked for the President by the Constitution. Powers of President can be summarized under following categories: -

1. EXECUTIVE POWERS

1. **Article 53** of the Constitution declares the President to be the chief of the state. Sub-clause (i) states, "The executive powers of the union shall be vested in the President and shall be exercised by him either directly or through offices sub-ordinate to him in accordance with his constitution. The Constitution vests the supreme executive authority of the Union in the President.

2. Under **Article 77**, all the executive actions of the government are taken under the name of the President.

3. He holds the **supreme command of India's defence forces** and has the power of declaring war or concluding peace.

4. Under **Article 78**, the President has the right to seek any information from the Centre and the State.

5. The President appoints, as Prime Minister, the person most likely to command the support of the majority in the Lok Sabha (usually the leader of the majority party or coalition). The President then appoints the other members of the Council of Ministers, distributing portfolios to them on the advice of the Prime Minister.

f. Under **Article 310**, every officer of the government occupies his/her position during the pleasure of the President.

g. It is the President of India by whom Houses of Parliament are summoned and he may convene joint sitting of the two Houses in case of deadlock.

h. The President **nominates 12 members for the Rajya Sabha** with extra-ordinary accomplishments from amongst persons who have special knowledge or practical experience in respect of such matters as literature, science, art and social service and **two members forthe Lok Sabha from the Anglo-Indian Community.**

i. The President is responsible for making a **wide variety of appointments**. These include:

  - Governors of States
  - The Chief Justice, other judges of the Supreme Court and High Courts of India
  - The Chief Minister of National capital territory of Delhi (Article 239 AA 5 of the constitution)
  - The Attorney General
  - The Comptroller and Auditor General
  - The Chief Election Commissioner and other Election Commissioners
  - The Chairman and other Members of the Union Public Service Commission
  - Vice Chancellor of central university and academic staff of central university through his nominee
  - Ambassadors and High Commissioners to other countries

j. Besides he has the power to **appoint an Inter-State Commission, Finance Commission,Election Commission, etc**. He has the power to be kept informed of all the officers of the Union. It is the duty of the Prime Minister to communicate to the President all decisions of the council of ministers relating to the administration of Union Affairs.

2. **LEGISLATIVE POWERS**

According to the Constitution, the President is an integral part of the Parliament. He has many powers in relation to the Parliament-

a. The President **inaugurates the Parliament by addressing it after the general elections**and also at the beginning of the first session each year. Presidential address on these occasions is generally meant to outline the new policies of the government. **[Article 87]**

b. He **summons, prorogues the Parliament.**

c. He **can dissolve the House of people.**

d. He **can address either Houses of Parliament or both the Houses jointly** (i.e., a joint session of both the houses of the Parliament).

e. He **can send message to either House of Parliament whether with respect to a Bill pending** in Parliament or otherwise. [Article 86(2)]

f. The President **decides questions as to disqualification of members. [Art. 103]**

g. He can **cause certain reports and statements to be laid before the Parliament** such as the report of the Comptroller and Auditor General, or the Report of the Finance Commission.

h. He **recommends the introduction of certain bills** in the Parliament such as the re- organization of states or alteration of boundaries; a money-bill involving expenditure.

i. **No bill can become a law unless and until assented to by the President. [Article 114]** All bills passed by the Parliament can become laws only after receiving the assent of the President. After a bill is presented to him, the President shall declare either that he assents to the Bill, or that he withholds his assent from it. As a third option, he can return a bill to the Parliament, if it is not a money bill or a Constitutional amendment bill, for reconsideration. When, after reconsideration, the bill is passed and presented to the President, with or without amendments, the President cannot withhold his assent from it. The President can also withhold his assent to a bill when it is initially presented to him (rather than return it to the Parliament) thereby exercising a pocket veto.

j. The President **may withhold his assent or return the Bill to the House, for reconsideration, if it is not a money bill.**

k. Certain types of bills passed by the state Legislature are to be reserved for Presidents' assent. Certain bills require his prior sanction before they are introduced in the state Legislature.

l. The most important legislative power of the President is his **power to promulgate _Ordinances_ under _Article 123_.** According to this, the President is empowered to promulgate ordinances, except when both the Houses of Parliament are in session, if he is satisfied that circumstances exit compelling him to take immediate action.

A Presidential Ordinance has the same force and effect as an Act of Parliament. However, every such ordinance should be laid before both Houses of Parliament within six weeks from the re-assembly of Parliament. Failure to comply with this condition, or Parliamentary disapproval within the six weeks' period, will make the Ordinance invalid. The President may also withdraw the Ordinance at any time he likes.

3. **FINANCIAL POWERS**

In respect of finance, the President enjoys the following powers:

a. **No money bill can be introduced in the House of people without the previous sanction of President.** All money bills originate in House of the people (Lok Sabha) **(Article 109).**
b. The president shall cause to be laid before Parliament, the **Annual Budget and supplementary Budget for its approval (Article 112).**
c. He causes to be laid before the Parliament the Annual Finance Statement called the **Budget before the beginning of every financial year.**
d. **Withdrawal from the Contingency Fund of India is done after the permission of the President.** The Contingency Fund of India is at the disposal of the President. He can make advances from the contingency fund of India to meet unforeseen expenses, pending approval by the Parliament.
e. The **President appoints the Finance Commission** from time to time to make recommendation regarding the distribution of taxes between the Union and the states.
f. He **determines the shares of Income Tax receipts between the Union and the States.**

4. **JUDICIAL POWERS (PARDONING POWER**

The President has the power to grant pardons and reprieves, and suspend, remit or commute sentences of persons convicted by court martial, and in all cases in which sentences of death have been passed. As mentioned in **Article 72** of Indian Constitution, the President is empowered with the powers to grant pardons in the following situations:

- Punishment is for offence against Union Law
- Punishment is by a Military Court
- Sentence is that of death

a. To pardon means to forgive a person of his offence. *It isan act of grace*and cannot be claimed or demanded as a matter of right. It is purely an executive act. The decisions involving pardoning and other rights by the President are independent of the opinion of the Prime Minister or the Lok Sabha majority. In most cases, however, the President exercises his executive powers on the advice of the Prime Minister and the cabinet.

The Presidents power does not affect the similar powers of the Governor and military officers with respect to Court-Martial. It is noteworthy that the Presidents' judicial power does not include the power to grant amnesty. This power is left to the Parliament.

b. **Advisory Jurisdiction under Article 143**also comes under judicial powers of the President.
c. The President enjoys certain ***privileges***in respect to criminal or civil proceedings against him. No criminal proceedings can be started against him during his term of office. Civil proceedings can be initiated only after he has been served with two months written notice.

5. MILITARY POWERS

The Supreme Command of the Defence Forces is vested in the President of India, but the Constitution expressly lay down that the exercise of this power shall be regulated by law.

This means that though the President may have the power to take action as to declaration of war or peace or the employment of the Defence Forces, it is competent for Parliament to regulate or control the exercise of such powers.

6. DIPLOMATIC POWERS

Like the head of other States, the President of India represents India in international affairs and has the power to appoint Indian representatives to other countries and receives diplomatic representatives of other states.

7. EMERGENCY POWERS

In addition to the power enumerated above the President of India enjoys vast emergency powers. ***Article 352 to 360***deals with the emergency provisions. The Constitution visualizes three kinds of emergencies: -

a. **Emergency arising out of a threat to the security of India or any part of it by war, external aggression or internal disturbances,**
b. **Emergency arising out of the failure of the constitutional machinery in any one of the states.**
c. **Emergency caused by a threat to the financial stability of India.**

It is the President who determines whether the emergency exists or not. His judgement in this case cannot be questioned. If the President issues a declaration of national emergency caused by war or threat of war he may: -

- **Suspend the autonomy of states and empower the Parliament to make laws on all matters including matters in the state list.**
- **Extend the executive power of the union so as to give directions to any state regarding the manner in which the executive power of the union is to be exercised;**
- **Suspend the fundamental rights including the right to constitutional remedies.**

- **The President can modify the provisions relating to distribution of revenues between the centre and the states in order to secure adequate revenue for the Government of India to meet situation created by emergency.**

The above is the assessment of various powers of the President of India. Looking to these powers one may say that President is no less than a dictator and especially so when an emergency has been declared.

However, whatever may be the Constitutional provisions regarding the powers of the President and however vast these powers may be, yet it may be said that the President of India being the head of a parliamentary Government cannot but exercise his powers on the advice of the Council of Ministers which includes the elected representatives of the people.

Article 74 clearly provides that "there shall be a Council of Ministers to aid and advice the President in the exercise of these functions. Article 74 is a mandatory provision.

The Constitution does not visualize the rule of the President at the centre. The powers of the President are the powers of the Council of Ministers which is responsible to the Parliament. The President must act according to their advice because disregard of their advice would kill the essence of the parliamentary Government which requires that the head of the state should exercise his powers on the advice of the cabinet responsible to the parliament.

VICE-PRESIDENT OF INDIA

The Vice-President is **elected under Article 63** of the Constitution. His importance in the Constitution is that whenever any vacancy occurs in the office of the President, he acts as President until a new President is elected. The Vice-President like the President is **elected indirectly**.

The Vice-President is elected by the members of both Houses of Parliament at a joint session by secret ballot in accordance with the system of proportional representation by means of single transferable vote.

The Vice-President of India shall be ex-officio Chairman of the Raba Sabha. His normal function is to preside over meetings of the Rajya Sabha. But since he is not the member of the Rajya Sabha, he has no right to vote.

QUALIFICATION

The qualifications of the Vice President are the *same as those of the President except that he __must be eligible for election to the Rajya Sabha__*.

i. He must be a citizen of India.
ii. He must have completed the age of 35 years.
iii. He must be eligible to be elected as a member of the Rajya Sabha.
iv. He must not hold any office of profit under any government.

ELECTION OF THE VICE-PRESIDENT

The Vice-President of India is elected by the members of both Houses of Parliament in accordance with the system of proportional representation by means of a single transferable vote system and the voting at such election shall be by secret ballot.

TERM OF OFFICE OF VICE-PRESIDENT

The Vice-President is elected for the term *__five years__*. The period of five years starts from the date on which he enters upon his office.

He is eligible for re-election. However, he may resign from his office before the expiry of normal term, even before the completion of his tenure by writing to President or may be removed by a resolution of the Rajya

Sabha passed by a simple majority of all the then members of the House and agreed to by a simple majority of the Lok Sabha.

FUNCTIONS OF THE VICE-PRESIDENT

The duties of the Vice-President are two-fold: -

1. He is the ex-officio chairman of the Rajya Sabha and
2. He acts for the President when the office of the President is vacant.

Even when the President is ill or otherwise unable to perform his duties, the Vice- President acts for him.

POSITION OF VICE-PRESIDENT

There is no doubt that the office of the Vice-President of India is next to the office of the President of India. But the Vice-President of India does not exercise any important and real powers. Therefore, the office of the Vice-President of India is not of any great importance.

XVIII
PARLIAMENT

The word *'Parliament'* is derived from the French word *'Parler'* *which means* *'to talk'*.

The term connotes a place where people sit and discuss national and international problems and enact legislation for their country.

THE UNION PARLIAMENT

THE PRESIDENT

THE TWO HOUSES

1. THE HOUSE OF PEOPLE(LOK SABHA)

2. THE COUNCIL OF STATES(RAJYA SABHA)

The Union Parliament of India consists of *the President* and *the two Houses known as the House of people and the Council of states*. The House of people is the Lower chamber where as the council of states is the upper chamber of the house of parliament.

The Rajya Sabha is composed many of representatives of the states elected by the State Assemblies. The Lok Sabha is composed of directly elected representatives on the basis of adult franchise and territorial constituencies. *The President is an integral part of the parliament.*

Under the Constitution of India, *the legislature of the Union is called Parliament* is the pivot on which the political system of the country revolves.

THE HOUSE OF PEOPLE (LOK SABHA)

The House of people is known as the *'Lower House'* of Parliament or the *'Lok Sabha'* Its members are elected directly by the people.

Composition of Lok Sabha

- 530 MEMBERS CHOSEN BY DIRECT ELECTION FROM TERRITORIAL CONSTITUENCIES IN THE STATE
- NOT MORE THAN 20 MEMBERS TO REPRESENT UNION TERRITORIES
- TWO MEMBERS OF THE ANGLO- INDIAN, COMMUNITY MAYBE NOMINATED BY THE PRESIDENT

Under the Constitution, **not more than 530 members** are to be chosen by direct election from territorial constituencies in the states, and **_not more than 20 members to represent the unionTerritories._**

In addition, **_two members of the Anglo-Indian, community maybe nominated by thePresident_**, if he is of the opinion that the community is not adequately represented in the Lok Sabha. Thus, the maximum strength of the House envisaged in the constitution is thus **552**.

The total elected strength of the Lok Sabha is distributed among the states in such a way that the ratio between the number of seats and the population of any state is as far as possible the same for all states. At present the Lok Sabha consists of 545 members.

Direct Election: The election to the Lok Sabha is **_conducted on the basis of adult franchise_**where every man or woman who has completed the age of 18 years is eligible to vote. The Constitution provides for secret ballot. According to the present system, a candidate who secures the largest number of votes is declared elected.

Duration of the Lok Sabha:

Lok Sabha has been provided with a **_fixed term_**as in the case of the popularly elected House of Representatives in the United States of America and the House of commons in the United Kingdom. The term of the Lok Sabha in India is **_five years from the date appointed for its first meeting._**

The expiration of the period of five years operates as its dissolution. The Lok Sabha may be dissolved before the expiration of its full term under certain circumstances, when a proclamation of Emergency is in force, the term of Lok Sabha can be extended by Parliament for a period not exceeding one year at a time and not exceeding in any case a period of six months after the proclamation has ceased to operate.

Qualifications for membership:

According to **_Article 84_**of the Constitution, following are the qualifications for the membership of Lok Sabha. A candidate must be-

a. a citizen of India;

b. have attained the age of twenty-five years and

c. must possess such other qualifications as may be prescribed by the parliament. A person holding an office of profit is disqualified from becoming a member of the House.

Sessions:

The Lok Sabha shall meet ***at least twice a year*** and ***the interval between two consecutive sessions shall be less than six months***. The time and place of meeting will be decided by the President who will summon the House to meet. He has also the power to prorogue the House.

THE COUNCIL OF STATES (RAJYA SABHA)

The Lok Sabha can also be summoned in a special session for disapproving the proclamation under Article 352, if a notice in writing signed by not less than one-tenth of the members of the Lok Sabha is given to the speaker. When such a notice is given the President must summon the session within 14 days.

The Rajya Sabha is the '***Upper House***' of Parliament and is sometimes called the '***House of Elders***'.

Composition of Rajya Sabha (Article 80):

- TWELVE MEMBERS TO BE NOMINATED BY THE PRESIDENT HAVING SPECIAL KNOWLEDGE OR PRACTICAL EXPERIENCE IN RESPECT OF LITERATURE, SCIENCE, ART AND SOCIAL SERVICE
- 250 MEMBERS NOT MORE THAN TWO HUNDRED AND THIRTY-EIGHT REPRESENTATIVES OF THE STATES AND OF THE UNION TERRITORIES.

The *present strength of the Rajya Sabha is 245* of these, *233 are elected by the various State Legislative Assemblies, thus making the Rajya Sabha predominantly an indirectly elected body.*

Indirect Election:

Whereas the Lok Sabha is directly elected on the basis of adult suffrage for five years, the Rajya Sabha is ***indirectly elected on a proportional representation basis by the state Legislatures.*** For the purpose of this election to each State is allotted a certain number of seats in the Rajya Sabha.

The main basis of such allotment is the strength of the population in each State. The members of each State Legislative Assembly from the electorate for the purpose of electing the requisite number of members allotted to each state thus ensuring the principle of State representation in the 'upper chamber' of parliament.

Another principle that is given recognition in the composition of the Rajya Sabha is representation of talent, experience and service. The method of proportional representation helps better representation of minorities.

Term of Upper House i.e., Rajya Sabha:

The Rajya Sabha enjoys a continuity of life. ***Under the Constitution, the Rajya Sabha cannot bedissolved.***The term of the members of the Rajya Sabha is six years and in this respect, it resembles the senate of the United States whose members are also chosen for six years.

In fact, the Rajya Sabha is a permanent body like the American Senate, *one third of themembers of the Rajya Sabha retire after every two years.*

Chairman and Deputy-Chairman of the Rajya Sabha-

The Vice-President of India is ex-officio chairman of the Rajya Sabha. He is elected by an electoral college consisting of the members of both the Lok Sabha and the Rajya Sabha.

While the office of the chairman is vacant, or during any period when the Vice- President acts as the President of India or discharges the functions of the President, the duties of the chairman of the Rajya Sabha are performed in the Deputy Chairman.

The Rajya Sabha also has a panel of members called Vice-Chairman' nominated by the chairman for the purpose of presiding over the Rajya Sabha in the absence of both the Chairman and Deputy Chairman.

POWERS OF THE PARLIAMENT

LEGISLATIVE POWERS

The Parliament is mainly a law-making organ. It can make laws on all the matters specified in the Union list and Concurrent list of the Seventh Schedule.

The State list is beyond the jurisdiction of the Union Parliament; but under certain circumstances it can also make laws on the subjects enumerated under this list. When the President has declared an emergency, the Parliament gets power to make law on the State list in normal times.

The Parliament can make laws on the State lists if:

a. The Council of States has declared by a resolution supported by not less than two-third of its members present and voting that it is necessary and expedient in the national interests that the Parliament should make laws with respect to any particular matter specified in the State list.

b. Two or more States request the Parliament to make a law on a particular subject for them;

c. Such a law is necessary for implementing any treaty, agreement or convention with any other country or countries or any decision made at any international conference, association or such other body.

EXECUTIVE POWERS

Under a Parliamentary Government, there being no strict separation of powers, the legislative organ controls the executive organ. The Parliament exercises control over the executive through numerous measures. It can move adjournment motions and can thereby bring to light the omissions and commissions of the administration.

It can put questions to the executive to elicit any information regarding administration. It can appoint investigation committees to go into any aspect of administration. In extreme cases, the Parliament can get rid of by passing a motion of no-confidence against it.

FINANCIAL POWERS

The Parliament controls the union purse. No taxes can be levied and no expenditure can be made by the Government without its approval. It determines the financial policy of the country.

CONSTITUENT POWERS

The Parliament has the power to amend the Constitution. It is worthy of note that while certain provisions of the Constitution may be amended without the consent of the States, none of the provisions can be amended without the approval of the Parliament.

There are some provisions of the Constitution which the Parliament can amend by a simple majority while certain others it can amend by a two-third majority. There are only a few matters which require the consent of the units.

DELIBERATIVE POWERS

The Parliament is also a debating assembly. It is the place where national questions are debated upon and policies are formulated. It is here that the actions of Government are reviewed and criticized. The discussion in the Parliament attracts the attention of the entire country and compels the Government to its intentions and policies.

MISCELLANEOUS POWERS

The Parliament constitutes a part of the electoral college to elect the President of India. It alone elects the Vice-President. It has the power to impeach the President.

It can recommend to the President the removal of other high officers of the State including the judges of the Supreme Court. Finally, the proclamation of Emergency by the President is subject to the approval of the parliament.

DISQUALIFICATIONSFOR THE MEMBERSHIPOF PARLIAMENT

a. No person shall be member of both the Houses of the Parliament.

b. No person shall be member of the Parliament and a State Assembly. The disqualification for the membership of Parliament is different thing from the disqualification for the membership. A person shall be disqualified for being chosen as a member of either House of Parliament—

c. If he holds an office of profit under the Govt. of India or the Government of any State.

d. If he is of unsound mind and stands so declared by a competent court.

e. If he is an undischarged insolvent.

f. If he is not a citizen of India.

g. If he acquires citizenship of any other State.

h. he shows allegiance to any other State.

i. If he is disqualified under any law made by the Parliament.

If any question arises as to disqualification of a member, the decision of President shall be final.

COUNCIL OF MINISTERS

Article 74of the Constitution of India provides that there would be a Council of Ministers with the ***Prime Minister as its head to aid and advise the President of the Indian Union in discharging hisduties.***

The Prime Minister is appointed by the President who also appoints other ministers on the advice of the Prime Minister.

The Council of Ministers is collectively responsible to the Lok Sabha. It is the duty of the Prime Minister to communicate to the President all decisions of the Council of Ministers relating to administration of the affairs of the Union and proposals for legislation and information relating to them.

The Council of Ministers comprises of ministers who are in three categories-

i. ***CABINET MEMBERS-*** Each member of the cabinet handles an independent charge of a department.

ii. **_MINISTERS OF STATE_**- They are also the ministers of the cabinet rank and help in discharging the duties of cabinet ministers.
iii. **_DEPUTY MINISTERS_**- They are the ministers of the lower rank and work under the state ministers.

THE PRIME MINISTER

The Constitution of India provides that there shall be a Council of Ministers to assist the President in discharging his duties. **_The Prime Minister of India heads the Council of Ministers._**

He is the leader of the party that enjoys a majority in the Lok Sabha. While the President of India is the head of the State, the Prime Minister is the head of the Government.

APPOINTMENT- The leader of the majority party in the Lok Sabha is appointed as the Prime Minister by the President. The President is the Constitutional head of the Union executive and the Prime Minister is the real head.

FUNCTIONS-

a. He selects other ministers, who are appointed by the President on the advice of the Prime Minister.
b. He presides over cabinet meetings.
c. He is the link between the President and the Cabinet It is the Prime Minister who keeps the President informed of the decisions of the Council of Ministers.
d. He guides the ministers and coordinates the policies of various departments and ministries.
e. He is the leader of the Lok Sabha in Parliament.
f. He is the Chairman of the Planning Commission.
g. He is the Chief confidential advisor to the President.

Term of the office-The term does **_not exceed five years_**. He may also be removed from his office when his party loses majority in Lok Sabha.

Resignation- If the government is defeated in the Lok Sabha, the Cabinet and the Prime Minister both have to resign as they are responsible to the Lok Sabha.

MONEY BILL

Article 110 of the Constitution **_defines Money Bill_**. It provides that-

1. For the purpose of this chapter, a Bill shall be deemed to be money bill if it contains only provisions dealing with all or any of the following matters, namely: -

   a. the imposition, abolition, remission, alteration or regulation of any tax;
   b. the regulation of the borrowing of money or the giving of any guarantee by the Government of India, or the amendment of the law with respect to any financial obligations undertaken or to be undertaken by the Government of India;
   c. the custody of the Consolidated Fund or the Contingency Fund of India, the payment of moneys into or the withdrawal of moneys from any such Fund;
   d. the appropriation of moneys out of the Consolidated Fund of India;
   e. the declaring of any expenditure to be expenditure charged on the Consolidated Fund of India or the increasing of the amount of any such expenditure;
   f. the receipt of money on account of the Consolidated Fund of India or the public account of India or the custody or issue of such money or the audit of the accounts of the Union or of a State; or
   g. any matter incidental to any of the matters specified in sub-clauses (a) to (f).

2. A Bill shall not be deemed to be a Money Bill by reason only that it provides for the imposition of fines or other pecuniary penalties, or for the demand or payment of fees for licenses or fees for services rendered, or by reason that it provides for the imposition, abolition, remission, alteration or regulation of any tax by any local authority or body for local purposes.

3. If any question arises whether a Bill is a Money Bill or not, the decision of the Speaker of the House of the People thereon shall be final.

4. There shall be endorsed on every Money Bill when it is transmitted to the Council of States under article 109, and when it is presented to the President for assent under article 111, the certificate of the Speaker of the House of the People signed by him that it is a Money Bill.

Procedure in respect of Money Bill-

A Money Bill shall not be introduced in the Council of States except on the recommendation of the President.

After a Money Bill has been passed by the house of the People it shall be transmitted to the Council of States for its recommendation and the Council of States shall within a period of fourteen days from the date of its receipt return the Bill to the House of the People with its recommendations and the House of the People may thereupon either accept or reject all or any of the recommendations of the Council of States. If the House of the People accepts any of the recommendations of the Council of States, the Money Bill shall be deemed to have been passed by both Houses with the amendments recommended by the Council of States and accepted by the House of the People

If the House of the People does not accept any of the recommendation, of the Council of States, the Money Bill shall be deemed to have been passed by both the Houses in the form in which it was passed by the House of the People without any of the amendments recommended by the Council of States.

If a Money Bill is passed by the House of the People and transmitted to the Council of States for its recommendations is not returned to the House of the People within the said period of fourteen days, it shall be deemed to have been passed by both Houses at the expiration of the said period in the form in which it was passed by the House of the People. ***[Art. 109]***

ORDINARY BILL

- Articles 107 & 108 deal with Ordinary Bills.
- An Ordinary Bill can be introduced any of the Houses of Parliament.
- An ordinary Bill can be introduced only with the recommendation of President.
- A dead-lock may occur.
- A Joint session of Houses may be 'lied to resolve the dead-look.
- When a Bill is passed in one House and it is sent to the other House for passing, the other House may keep that Bill for six months with it.
- The House has to oblige the recommendations of the other House.
- Certificate from the Speaker's not necessary.

MONEY BILL

- Articles 109 and 110 deal with Money Bills

- A Money Bill can only be introduced in the Lok Sabha.
- The Money Bill can be introduced without the recommendations of the President.
- No deadlock occurs
- Joint session of the Houses is not necessary.
- A Money Bill is always passed by Lok Sabha. Thereafter it is sent to Rajya Sabha for recommendations. It can keep only for 14 days.
- Lok Sabha may consider or may not consider the recommendations of the Rajya Sabha pertaining to Money Bills.
- The Speaker has to give a certificate for the Money Bill.

XIX

SUPREME COURT

In a democratic set-up like India, judiciary is the supreme authority in the sense that it is the guardian of the Constitution and the rights of the citizens. Also, it has been vested with the duty to strike a balance between the central government and the governments of the federating units, other pillars of the democracy. Therefore, existence of an independent and impartial judiciary is an essential pre-requisite of a federal form of government. It acts as the custodian of democracy and the guardian of the rights and liberties of the people.

Unlike other federal systems, we do not have separate hierarchies of federal and state courts. For the entire Republic of India, there is one unified judicial system- one hierarchy of courts- with the Supreme Court as the highest or the apex court. Then there are High Courts at the state level and subordinate courts below them.

The Supreme Court of India consists of the Chief Justice and 30 other judges, appointed by the president. The Parliament has the power to prescribe the number of judges and no formal amendment of the constitution is required for this purpose.

Article 124provides for the ***establishment and constitution of Supreme Court-***

1. There shall be a Supreme Court of India consisting of a Chief Justice of India and, until Parliament by law prescribes a larger number, of not more than 30 Judges.
2. Every Judge of the Supreme Court shall be appointed by the President by warrant under his hand and seal after consultation with such of the

Judges of the Supreme Court and of the High Courts in the States as the President may deem necessary for the purpose and ***shall hold office until he attains theage of sixty-five years***:

Provided thatin the case of appointment of a Judge other than the Chief Justice, the Chief Justice of India shall always be consulted:
Provided further that—

a. a Judge may, by writing under his hand addressed to the President, resign his office;
b. a Judge may be removed from his office in the manner provided in clause (4).

QUALIFICATIONS AND SALARY
For appointment as a judge of the Supreme Court a person must be-

a. Must be a citizen of India, and
b. has been for at least five years a Judge of a High Court or of two or more such Courts in succession; or
c. has been for at least ten years an advocate of a High Court or of two or more such Courts in succession; or
d. is, in the opinion of the President, a distinguished jurist.

Thus, a non-practicing or an academic lawyer may also be appointed as a judge of the Supreme Court if he is, in the opinion of the President, a distinguished jurist.

Provision has also been made for the appointment of a judge of a High Court as ad hoc judge of the Supreme Court and retired judges of the Supreme Court or of High Court to sit and act as judge of the Supreme Court. The Constitution debars a retired judge of Supreme Court from practicing in any court of law or before any other authority in India. The salary of the judges is charged upon the Consolidated Fund of India.

REMOVAL OF JUDGES
The judges of the Supreme Court can be removed from office by the President only after an address by each house of Parliament supported by more than two thirds majority of members present and voting has been presented to the President in the same session for removal of the judges on the ground of proved misbehavior or incapacity.

Oath - Every person appointed as a judge of the Supreme Court before he enters upon his office, takes an oath before the President or some person appointed in that behalf by him in the form prescribed in the Constitution. The Constitution prohibits a person who has hold office as a judge of the Supreme Court from practicing law before any court in the territory of India (Art 124 (6) and (7)).

The Constitution prohibits a person who has held office as a Judge of the Supreme Court from practicing or acting as a judge in any court or before any authority within the territory of India. But under **_Article 128_**, the _Chief Justice may appoint the retired judges to act as ad hoc judges in the Supreme Court._

Appointment of ad hoc judges and his qualification-

_Article 127_of the Constitution prescribes for the appointment and qualifications of the ad hoc

Judges.

It reads as under-

If at any time there should not be a quorum of the Judges of the Supreme Court available to hold or continue any session of the Court, the Chief Justice of India may, with the previous consent of the President and after consultation with the Chief Justice of the High Court concerned, request in writing the attendance at the sittings of the Court, as an ad hoc Judge, for such period as may be necessary, of a Judge of High Court duly qualified for appointment as a Judge of the Supreme Court to be designated by the Chief Justice of India.

It shall be the duty of Judge who has been so designated, in priority to other duties of his Office, to attend the sittings of the Supreme Court at the time and for the period for which his attendance is required, and while so attending he shall have all the jurisdiction, powers and privileges, and shall discharge the duties of a Judge of the Supreme Court.

JURISDICTION OF SUPREME COURT
ORIGINAL JURISDICTION (ARTICLE 131)

This refers to the cases that directly originate in the Supreme Court. It has original exclusive jurisdiction in any dispute between-

a. the Government of India and one or more States; or
b. the Government of India and any State or States on one side and one or more other States on the other; or
c. two or more States.

Such a dispute should, however, involve some question of law or fact on which the existence or extent of a legal right depends. The treaties concluded between the Centre and the princely states are excluded from the Court's original jurisdiction

The President may, however, refer the above-mentioned disputes to the Supreme Court for opinion and the Supreme Court shall, after such hearing as it thinks fit, report to the President its opinion thereon.

Article 32empowers the Supreme Court to issue directions or orders in the nature of the writs of habeas corpus, mandamus, prohibition, quo warranto and certiorari, or any of them, for the enforcement of fundamental rights. It is to be noted that this jurisdiction is not exclusive. It is concurrent. High Courts of States have also been granted similar powers.

Art 139also empowers the Supreme Court with exactly similar powers. It says-

"Parliament, by law, may confer on the Supreme Court, power to issue directions, orders or writs including writs in the nature of habeas corpus, mandamus, prohibition, quo warranto and certiorari or any of them.

Under the scheme of the Constitution, ***Article 131***confers original jurisdiction on the Supreme Court in regard to a dispute between two States of the Union of India or between one or more States and the Union of India.

APPELLATE JURISDICTION (ARTICLES 132 TO 136)

This refers to the power of reviewing and revising the orders of lower courts and tribunals. This jurisdiction extends to both the civil and the criminal appeals from the High Courts under certification from these courts or, in its absence, permitted by the Supreme Court itself. Normally, these appeals are in cases involving substantial question of law of general importance or interpretation of the Constitution or death penalty awarded by a High Court.

The Appellate jurisdiction of the Supreme Court extends to three branches:

A. **Civil,**
B. **Criminal, and (C) Constitutional.**

CIVIL APPELLATE JURISDICTION (ART. 133)

1. An appeal shall lie to the Supreme Court from any judgment, decree or final order in a civil proceeding of a High Court in the territory of India

if the High Court certifies under article 134A—

a. that the case involves a substantial question of law of general importance; and
b. that in the opinion of the High Court the said question needs to be decided by the Supreme Court.

2. Notwithstanding anything in article 132, any party appealing to the Supreme Court under clause (1) may urge as one of the grounds in such appeal that a substantial question of law as to the interpretation of this Constitution has been wrongly decided.
3. Notwithstanding anything in this article, no appeal shall, unless Parliament by law otherwise provides, lie to the Supreme Court from the judgment, decree or final order of one Judge of a High Court.

CRIMINAL APPELLATE JURISDICTION (SEC. 134)

According to Article 134 an appeal lies to the Supreme Court from any judgment, final order or sentence in a criminal proceeding of a High Court in the following two ways-

1. with a certificate of the High Court, or
2. without a certificate of the High Court.

*1. **With a certificate of the High Court**—* Under clause (e) an appeal lies to the Supreme Court if the High Court certifies under Article 134-A (Added by 44th Amendment, 1978) that it is a fit case for appeal to the Supreme Court. [Art 134(c)]

Under the new Art. 134-A the High Court can grant a certificate for appeal to the Supreme Court tinder An. 132 either on its own motion or on 'oral' application of the aggrieved party immediately after passing the judgment, decree, or final order. Prior to this, the High Court does so only on the application of the aggrieved party. Under new Article (134-A); it can now grant a certificate on its own motion if it deems fit.

2. ***Without a certificate of the High Court***— An appeal lies to the Supreme Court without the certificate of the High Court if the High Court —

a. has on appeal reversed an order of acquittal of an accused person and sentenced him to death, or

b. has withdrawn for trial before itself, any case from any Court subordinate to its authority and has in such trial convicted the accused person and sentenced him to death. But if the High Court has reversed the order of conviction and has ordered the acquittal of an accused, no appeal would lie to the Supreme Court.

POWER OF PRESIDENT TO CONSULT SUPREME COURT(ADVISORY JURISDICTION) (Art. 143)

1. If at any time it appears to the President that a question of law or fact has arisen, or is likely to arise, which is of such a nature and of such public importance that it is expedient to obtain the opinion of the Supreme Court upon it, he may refer the question to that Court for consideration and the Court may, after such hearing as it thinks fit, report to the President its opinion thereon.

2. The President may, notwithstanding anything in the proviso to article 131, refer a dispute of the kind mentioned in the said proviso to the Supreme Court for opinion and the Supreme Court shall, after such hearing as it thinks fit, report to the President its opinion thereon.

The use of the word '*may*' in Art.143(1) indicates that the Supreme Court is not bound to answer a reference made to it by the President.

SUPREME COURT AS A COURT OF RECORD (ART. 129)

The Supreme Court shall be a Court of record and shall have all powers of such a Court, including the power to punish for contempt of itself. As a Court of record, it has the power to punish those who are adjudged as guilty of contempt of court.

APPEAL BY SPECIAL LEAVE (SEC. 136)

This power has been conferred upon the Supreme Court by Article 136. It may, in its discretion, grant special leave to appeal from any judgments, decree, determination, sentence or order in any cause or matter passed or made by any court or tribunal in the territory of India.

WRIT JURISDICTION (ART. 32)

The Supreme Court is the guardian of the individual liberties and fundamental rights. It has the power to declare a law passed by any legislature null and void if it encroaches upon the fundamental rights guaranteed to the people by the Constitution. For the enforcement of fundamental rights, it can issue writs in the nature of ***Habeas Corpus, Mandamus, Certiorari, Prohibition and Qua-Warranto.***

Besides the above-mentioned powers, the Supreme Court has the ***power of judicial review underArt.13***. It implies the power to review and determine validity of a law or an order. It refers to "the power of a court to inquire whether a law, executive order or other official action conflicts with the written Constitution, and if the court concludes that it does, to declare it unconstitutional and void".

However, the Indian Constitution does not in so many words assign the power of judicial review to the court. There are several specific provisions in the Constitution, which guarantee judicial review of legislation such as Articles 13, 32, 131-136, 143, 226, 145, 246, 251, 254 and 372.

Apart from these Articles, the power of judicial review is derived from the position of Supreme Court as the guardian of the Constitution.

The court can challenge the constitutional validity of a law on the following grounds:

a. the subject matter of the legislation is not within competence of the legislature which has passed it;
b. It is repugnant to the provisions of the Constitution; or
c. It infringes one of the fundamental rights.

The power of judicial review, in general, flows from the powers of the courts to interpret the Constitution. As such it has the final say in the interpretation of the Constitution and by such interpretation; the Supreme Court has extended its power of judicial review to almost all the provi- sions of the Constitution.

The limitations on the power of judicial review of the Supreme Court:

Under Article 137, the Supreme Court has expressly been given the power to review its judgment. However, this is subject to any law passed by the Parliament. This power is exercisable under rules made by the Court under Article 145, on grounds mentioned in Order 47, Rule 1 of C. P. C., a review will lie in the Supreme Court on-

1. Discovery of new and important matter or evidence;
2. Mistake or error apparent on the face of the record; and
3. Any other sufficient reason.

Article 141 of the Constitution provides that the judgment of the Supreme Court will be binding on all Courts in India.

MAINTENANCE OF INDEPENDENCE OF JUDICIARY

Only an impartial and independent judiciary can protect the rights of the individual and provide equal justice without force and fear. It is very necessary that the Supreme -Court should be allowed to function without fear and political pressure. There must be security of tenure of the judges, no alteration in the salaries during the term of their office etc. to enable a judge to administer justice freely.

The Constitution has made the following provisions to ensure the independence of judiciary—

a. ***Security of Tenure***—The Judges of the Supreme Court have security of tenure. They cannot be removed from their office except by an order of the President and that also on the ground of proved misbehavior or incapacity supported by a resolution adopted by a majority of total membership of each House and also by a majority of not less than 2/3 of the members of the House present and voting. Parliament may, however, regulate the procedure for presentation of the address and for investigation and proof of misbehavior or incapacity of a Judge. But Parliament cannot misuse this power because the special procedure for their removal must be followed.

b. ***Salaries etc. are fixed***—The salaries of the Judges of the Supreme Court and High Court are fixed by the Constitution and charged on the Consolidated Fund of India. They are not subject to vote of legislature. During the term of their office, their salaries and allowances cannot be altered to their disadvantage except in grave financial emergency.

c. ***Jurisdiction of Supreme Court not to be curtailed***—In respect of its jurisdiction, Parliament may change pecuniary limit for appeals to the Supreme Court, confer supplementary power to enable it to work more effectively, confer power to issue directions, orders or writs including all the prerogative writs for any purpose other than those mentioned in Art. 132. In this respect, the Parliament can extend but cannot curtail die jurisdiction of Supreme Court.

d. **No discussion in Legislature**—Neither in Parliament nor in a State Legislature a discussion can take place with respect to the conduct of a Judge of the Supreme Court in discharge of his duties.

e. **<u>Appointment of Judges</u>**—The Constitution does not leave the appointment of the Judges of the Supreme Court to the unguided discretion of the Executive. The Executive is required to consult Judges of the Supreme Court and High Courts in the appointment of the Judges of the Supreme Court.

Thus, the position of the Supreme Court is very strong and its independence is adequately guaranteed.

XX
CONSTITUTIONAL AMENDMENT

What is an amendment of constitution?

An amendment of Constitution is an improvement, a correction or a revision to the original content approved in 1788. As of January 2020, there have been 104 amendments of Constitution of India since it was first enacted in 1950.

The Constitution of India which was adopted by the Constituent Assembly on November 26, 1949 and it came into force on January 26, 1950. The framers of the constitution felt that this should be in accordance with the aspirations of the people and changes in the society. They did not see it as a sacred, stable and unwavering law. Therefore, they made provisions to incorporate changes from time to time. These changes are called constitutional amendments.

What is article 368 of Indian constitution?

Part-XX Article 368 (1) of the Constitution of India empowers constituent powers to make formal amendments and empowers Parliament to make changes or repeals, in addition to any provision as per the procedure laid down herein, which is different from the ordinary. The process of law is amended in Article 368 by the 24th and 42nd Amendments in 1971 and 1976 respectively.

There are three types of amendments to the Constitution of India in which second and third type of amendments are governed by Article 368.

1. The first type of amendments includes that can be passed by "simple majority" in each house of the Parliament of India.

2. The second type of amendments includes that can be effected by the parliament by a prescribed "special majority" in each house; and

3. The third type of amendments includes those that require, in addition to such "special majority" in each house of the parliament, ratification by at least one half of the State Legislatures.

Under Indian Constitution Article 368 of Part XX provides for two types of amendments: –

- **By a special majority of the parliament:**

It refers to the majority of $2/3^{rd}$ members present and voting. It is used to pass a Rajya Sabha resolution empowering Parliament to enact legislation in the state list. It refers to the majority of $2/3^{rd}$ members present and voting at more than 50% of the total strength of the House. It is mainly used for most of the constitution amendment bill. Examples where a majority of this type is used: –

1. Passing a constitutional amendment bill that does not affect federalism.
2. Removal of judges of Supreme Court or High Court.
3. Removal of Comptroller and Auditor General (CAG) or Chief Election Commissioner (CEC) of India.
4. National emergency
5. Resolution by the State Legislature for the abolition or creation of the Legislative Council.

With a special majority of Parliament ratified by half of the total states:
The provisions of the Constitution which pertain to the federal structure of the polity can be amended by a special majority of Parliament as well as by simple majority with the consent of half of the state legislators. If one or some or all of the remaining states take no action on the bill, it does not matter; half of the states gave their consent, the formality being completed. There is no time limit within which states should give their consent to the bill. These provisions can be amended: –

1. Election of President and its manner.
2. Extension of executive power of the Union and the States.

3. Supreme Court and High Court.
4. Distribution of legislative powers between
5. Union and States.
6. Any list in the Seventh Schedule.
7. Representation of States in Parliament.
8. Power of Parliament to amend the Constitution and its procedure (Article 368 itself).

Procedure of Amendment of Constitution as per Article 368

According to Article 368, the procedure for amendment of the Constitution is as follows in Article 368: –

A constitutional amendment can be initiated only with the introduction of a bill in any House of Parliament (Lok Sabha and Rajya Sabha) and not in state legislatures.

The Bill can be introduced by a Minister or a private member and does not require prior permission of the President.

The Bill must be passed by a special majority in each House, that is, a majority of the total membership of the House (i.e. more than 50 per cent) and a majority of the two-thirds of the current members of the House and voting.

Each House has to pass a separate bill.

In case of disagreement between the two Houses, there is no provision for holding a joint sitting of the two Houses for deliberation and passing the Bill.

If the bill seeks to amend the federal provisions of the Constitution, it must be approved by a simple majority by the legislators of half the states, namely, presence and voting of the majority of the members of the House.

After being duly passed by both the Houses of Parliament and ratified by the State Legislatures, the Bill is presented to the President where necessary.

After the President's assent, the bill becomes an Act (i.e., a Constitution Amendment Act) and is amended according to the terms of the Constitution Act.

Some important Amendments of Indian Constitution

1. First Amendment Act, 1951

- Added special provision for the advancement of any socially and economically backward classes or for the Scheduled Castes and Scheduled Tribes (SCs and STs). To fully secure the constitutional validity of zamindari abolition laws and to place reasonable restriction on freedom of speech. A new constitutional device, called Schedule 9 introduced to protect against laws that are contrary to the Constitutionally guaranteed fundamental rights. These laws encroach upon property rights, freedom of speech and equality before law.

- Empowering the state to make special provisions for the advancement of socially and economically backward classes. Provided for the saving of laws provided for the acquisition of estates etc.
- The Ninth Schedule was added to protect land reform and other laws therein from judicial review. Article 31 was followed by Articles 31A and 31B.

2. The Constitution (Seventh Amendment of Constitution) Act, 1956

- Reorganisation of states on linguistic lines, abolition of Class A, B, C, D states and introduction of Union territories.
- The Seventh Amendment brought the most comprehensive changes to the constitution ever. This amendment was made to implement the State Reorganization Act.
- The Second and Seventh Schedules were substantially amended for the purpose.

3. The Constitutional (10th Amendment of Constitution) Act, 1961

- Incorporation of Dadra and Nagar Haveli as a Union Territory, consequent to acquisition from Portugal.
- The Tenth Amendment unifies the territories of the free Dadra and Nagar Haveli with the Union of India and provides for their administration under the regulation of the powers to form a President.

4. The Constitutional (13th Amendment of Constitution) Act, 1963

- Formation of State of Nagaland, with special protection under Article 371A.
- Gave Nagaland the status of a state and made special provisions for it to the States Reorganization Act.

5. The Constitution (24th Amendment of Constitution) Act, 1971

- Enable parliament to dilute fundamental rights through amendments to the constitution.
- Articles 13 and 368 were amended to remove all possible doubts regarding the power of Parliament to amend the constitution and procedure.
- It exercises authority over Golak Nath and asserts the power of Parliament, Golak Nath was rejected to amend the fundamental rights.

6. The Constitution (Twenty-fifth) Amendment Act, 1971

- Restrict property rights and compensation in case the state takes over private property. However, the Supreme Court quashed a part of Article 31C, to the extent it took away the power of judicial review. This was done in the landmark case of Kesavananda Bharati vs. State of Kerala (1973) 4 SCC 225 which for the first time enunciated the Basic structure doctrine.
- The 25th Amendment of the Constitution in 1971 added a new section to Article 31C in the Constitution. By the 1971, the position of the fundamental rights was higher than Directive Principles of State.
- Article 31C sought to change the relationship to some extent by citing preeminence over Articles 14, 19 and 31 over Articles 14 (b) and 39 (c).

7. Twenty-sixth Amendment of Constitution Act, 1971

- Abolition of privy purse paid to former rulers of princely states which were incorporated into the Indian Republic.
- Abolished privy purses and privileges of former rulers of princely states.

8. The Constitution (Thirty-second Amendment) Act, 1974

- Protection of regional rights in Telangana and Andhra regions of State of Andhra Pradesh.
- This amendment added twenty state enactments relating to land sealing and land tenure reforms to the Ninth Schedule of the Constitution.

9. The Constitution (Thirty-eighth Amendment of Constitution) Act, 1975

- Enhances the powers of President and Governors to pass ordinances.
- Declaration of Emergency by the President made non-justification.

- The declaration of ordinances by the Presidents, Governors and Administrators of the Union Territories was held to be unjustified.
- Empowered the President to declare various proclamations of national emergency on different grounds simultaneously.

10. The Constitution (42nd Amendment of Constitution) Act, 1976:

- The amendment was meant to increase the power of the government. The major amendments made to the Constitution by the 42nd Amendment Act are as follows: –
- Amendment passed during internal emergency by Indira Gandhi. Provides for curtailment of fundamental rights, imposes fundamental duties and changes to the basic structure of the constitution by making India a "Socialist Secular" Republic. However, the Supreme Court, in Minerva Mills v. Union of India, quashed the amendments to Articles 31C and 368 as it was in contravention with the basic structure of the Constitution.
- The preamble has been changed to 'Sovereign Democratic Republic of India as 'Sovereign Socialist Secular Democratic Republic'.
- The term 'Unity of the nation' has been changed to integrity 'Unity and Integrity of the nation'.
- Parliament and State Legislative Assemblies: – The life span of the Lok Sabha and State Legislative Assemblies was extended from 5 to 6 years.
- Executive: – It expressly amends Article 74 of the State that the President shall act in accordance with the advice of the Council of Ministers in the discharge of his functions.
- Judiciary: – The 42nd Amendment Act inserted
- Article 144A and Article 128A, the creators of the Constitutional Amendment Act further innovated in the field of judicial review of the constitutional review of legislation.
- Federalism: – The Act has added Article 257A to the Constitution so that the Center can deploy any armed force, or any other force of the Union, to deal with the critical situation of law and order in any state.
- Fundamental Rights and Directive Principles: – A major change that was made by the 42nd Constitutional Amendment was to give priority to all the Directive Principles on Fundamental Rights contained in Articles 14, 19 or 31.

- Fundamental Duties: – The 42nd Amendment Act inserted Article 51-A to create a new part called IV-A in the Constitution, which laid down fundamental duties to the citizens.
- Emergency: – Before the 42nd Amendment Act, the President could declare an emergency under Article 352 all over the country and not in one part of the country alone. The Act authorized the President to declare an emergency in any part of the country.

Evolution of the Basic Structure Concept

The concept of the basic structure of the Constitution evolved over time. In this section, we will discuss this development with the help of some historical decisions related to this theory.

Shankari Prasad Case (1951)

In this case, the SC argued that the power of Parliament to amend the Constitution under Article 368 also included the power to amend the Fundamental Rights guaranteed in Part III.

Sajjan Singh case (1965)

In this case also, the SC considered that Parliament can amend any part of the Constitution including fundamental rights.

It is worth mentioning that two disgruntled judges commented on whether the fundamental rights of citizens in Parliament could become the role of a majority party.

Golaknath case (1967)

In this case, the court reversed its earlier stance that fundamental rights could be amended.

It stated that Article 13 states that fundamental rights are not liable to parliamentary restriction and a new Constituent Assembly would be required to amend fundamental rights.

It was also stated that Article 368 gives the procedure for amending the Constitution but does not give Parliament the power to amend the Constitution. The case awarded the fundamental rights 'transcendental position'.

The majority decision invoked the concept of inherent limitations on the power of Parliament to amend the constitution. According to this view, the Constitution gives stability to the basic freedom of the citizens.

In giving themselves the constitution, the people had secured these rights for themselves.

Kesavananda Bharti Case (1973)

This was a historical case in defining the concept of basic structure theory.

The SC considered that although no part of the constitution, including fundamental rights, is beyond the amended power of Parliament, "the basic structure of the constitution cannot also be repealed by constitutional amendment."

The decision implied that Parliament could only amend the constitution and not rewrite it. It is just a power to amend and not the power to destroy.

This is the basis in Indian law in which the judiciary can repeal any amendment passed by Parliament which is in conflict with the basic structure of the Constitution.

Indira Nehru Gandhi vs. Raj Narayan case (1975)

Here, the SC applied the principle of basic structure and struck down clause (4) of Article 329-A, which was inserted by the 39th Amendment in 1975 on the ground that it was beyond the amended power of the Parliament as it destroy the amending powers of the parliament.

The 39th Amendment Act was passed by the Parliament during the Emergency. The Act elected the President, Vice President, Prime Minister and Speaker of the Lok Sabha beyond the scrutiny of the judiciary.

Minerva Mills Case (1980)

This case again reinforces the basic structure theory. The 42nd Amendment Act 1976 ruled on 2 changes to the constitution, declaring them to be infringing on the basic structure.

The decision makes it clear that not the parliament but the constitution is supreme.

In this case, the court added two features to the list of basic infrastructure facilities. They were: judicial review and balance between fundamental rights and the DPSP.

Waman Rao Case (1981)

The SC reiterated the basic structure principle again.

It drew a line of demarcation as the date of the verdict of Keshvananda Bharti on April 24, 1913, and held that it should not be retrospectively applied to reopen the validity of any amendment to the constitution that preceded that date. Should not be done.

In the Kesavananda Bharati case, the petitioner challenged the Constitution (29th Amendment) Act, 1972, which placed the Kerala Land Reforms Act, 1963 and its amended Act in the 9th Schedule to the Constitution.

Waman Rao case verdict states that the amendments made to the 9th schedule and the cases passed after that date may be subject to scrutiny till the Kesavananda decision is valid.

Indra Sawhney and Union of India (1992)

The SC examined the scope and extent of Article 16 (4), which provides for reservation of jobs in favor of backward classes. It retained the constitutional validity of 27% reservation for OBCs with certain conditions (e.g. creamy layer boycott, no reservation in promotion, total reserved quota should not exceed 50%, etc.)

Here, the 'Rule of Law' was added to the list of basic features of the Constitution.

S. R. Bommai Case (1994)

In this decision, the SC tried to prevent widespread misuse of Article 356 (in relation to imposition of President's rule for the states.

In this case, there was no question of constitutional amendment, but still, the concept of the basic principle was applied.

The Supreme Court held that state government policies directed against an element of the basic structure of the Constitution would be a valid basis for the exercise of central power under Article 356.

Doctrine of Basic Structure

According to the Indian Constitution, the Parliament and the State Legislatures can make laws within their jurisdictions. The power to amend the Constituiton is only with the parliament and not the state legislature assemblies. However, this power of the parliament is not absolute. the Supreme Court has the power declare any law that it finds unconstitutional void. As per the Basic Structure Doctrine, any amendment that tries to change the basic structure of the constitution is invalid.

In the Indian Constitution, the word basic structure is nowhere mentioned. The idea that Parliament cannot enforce laws that will develop slowly and in many cases over time in the basic structure of the Constitution. The idea is to uphold the nature of Indian democracy and to protect the rights and freedoms of the people. This principle helps to protect and preserve the spirit of the constitution document.

It was the Kesavananda Bharati case that brought this theory to the headlines. It was held that "the basic structure of the constitution cannot revoked even by constitutional amendment".

The decision listed some basic structures of the constitution: –

- Supremacy of the constitution
- Unity and sovereignty of India
- Democratic and republican form of government
- Federal character of constitution
- Secular character of constitution
- Separation of power
- Personal freedom

XXI

EMERGENCY PROVISION

Introduction

Black law's dictionary defines emergency "as a failure of the social system to deliver reasonable conditions of life". An emergency may be defined as "circumstances arising suddenly that calls for immediate action by the public authorities under the powers granted to them."

In India, the emergency provisions are such that the constitution enables the federal government to acquire the strength of unitary government whenever the situation demands. All the pacific methods should be exhausted during such situation and emergency should also be the last weapon to use as it affects India's federal feature of government.

There are three types of emergencies under the Indian Constitution namely-

1. National Emergency
2. State Emergency
3. Financial Emergency

National Emergency

Article 352 of the Constitution provides for the provision of National Emergency which can be applied if any extraordinary situation arises that may threaten the security, peace, stability and governance of the country.

Whenever any of the following grounds occur, an emergency can be imposed:

1. War,
2. External aggression; or
3. Internal rebellion.

Article 352 provides that if the President is 'satisfied' on the grounds that the security of India is threatened due to outside aggression or armed rebellion, he can issue a proclamation to that effect regarding the whole of India or a part thereof.

However, sub-clause (3) states that when a piece of written advice is given by the Union Cabinet then only the President can make such a proclamation. Such a proclamation must be placed before each house of the parliament and must be approved within one month of the declaration of the proclamation otherwise it will expire.

Furthermore, it is not necessary that for the proclamation of National emergency, external aggression or armed rebellion should actually happen. Even if there is a possibility that such a situation can arise, a national emergency can be proclaimed.

In **Minerva Mills vs Union of India**, it has been held that there can be no bar to judicial review of determining the validity of the proclamation of emergency issued by the President under Article 352(1). The court's powers are limited only to examining whether the limitations conferred by the Constitution have been observed or not. It can check if the satisfaction of President is on valid grounds or not. If the President is satisfied that grounds for national emergency exist but the same is based on absurd, malafide or irrelevant grounds then it won't be considered that the President is 'satisfied'.

Procedure for revoking emergency

If the situation improves then the President can revoke the emergency through another proclamation. The 44th Amendment of the Constitution provides that a requisition for the meeting can be made by ten per cent or more members of the Lok Sabha and in that meeting; it can disapprove or revoke the emergency by a simple majority. The emergency will immediately become inoperative in such a case.

Territorial Extent of Proclamation

The President may make a Proclamation of Emergency in respect of the whole India or any part of India, as required.

Duration of Emergency

If approved by both houses of Parliament then National Emergency can continue for 6 months and it can be renewed by approval of Parliament after every 6 months.

But if the dissolution of Lok Sabha takes place in that 6 months and resolution for renewal of National Emergency is under consideration then emergency exists till 30 days from the first sitting of newly elected LS provided that it is approved by Rajya Sabha.

Until 44th amendment 1978, if Parliament approves proclamation of National Emergency then it remains in operation on pleasure or desire of cabinet or executive.

Any of the above resolution related to proclamation or renewal of National Emergency must be passed by both houses of Parliament by a special majority (i.e. the majority of the total membership of that house or not less than 2/3rd of members present and voting). This provision is added by 44th amendment 1978 and before that such resolution can be passed by simple majority i.e. more than total members present and voting.

Effects of Proclamation of Emergency

1) Executive

While a Proclamation of Emergency is in operation, Union can use its executive power to the extent of giving directions to the State relating to the manner in which the executive powers shall be exercised by the State. The Constitution (42nd Amendment) Act 1976 made a consequential change in Article 353.

It states that the executive power of the Union to give directions and to make laws shall extend to other States too apart from the state where an emergency has been proclaimed and is in operation. The above-mentioned power shall be exercised if the security of India or any part of its territory is threatened by the activities in the part of the territory of India in which emergency has been proclaimed and is in operation.

In normal times, the power of the executive does not extend to giving such directions subject to certain exceptions.

2) Legislative

When an emergency has been proclaimed, the Parliament shall have the power to legislate as regards to State List (List II) as well. The emergency suspends the distribution of legislative powers between the Union and State and not the state legislature.

3) Financial

The centre is empowered to alter the distribution of revenue between the Union and the State.

While a Proclamation of Emergency is in operation, the President may, by order define the financial arrangement between the State and the Union as provided by Articles 268 to 279. Such order shall be laid before each House of Parliament and when the Proclamation of Emergency ceases to operate, such order shall too come to an end.

4) Extension Life of Lok Sabha

The normal life of Lok Sabha can be extended while a proclamation of emergency is in operation. Such an extension can be done by the Parliament for a period not exceeding one year at a time and not beyond a period of six months in any case after the Proclamation has ceased to operate.

5) Suspension of Fundamental Rights guaranteed by Article 19

Article 358 of the Indian Constitution provides for Suspension of fundamental freedoms guaranteed to the citizens by Article 19 of the Indian Constitution.

It provides that when an emergency has been proclaimed and is in operation, the provisions contained in article 19 shall not restrict the power of the State relating to the making of any law or taking any executive action which abridges or takes away the rights guaranteed by Article 19.

It means that the freedom guaranteed by Article 19 automatically stands suspended once the Proclamation of Emergency is made. Once the proclamation of emergency ceases to operate, Article 19 which stood suspended during the emergency automatically comes to life.

Suspension of the right of enforcement of fundamental rights (Art. 359)

A.D.M. Jabalpur v. S. Shukla, AIR 1976 SC 1207

This case is also known as the Habeas Corpus (to produce the body) case as whenever someone is arrested, this is the writ filed in the Supreme Court by the arrested person. Earlier, when the Proclamation of Emergency was made, this writ was not considered as a fundamental right under Article 21 and remained suspended.

The facts of the case were that on 26th June 1975 emergency was proclaimed by the President of India due to internal disturbances. The said proclamation was followed by another proclamation on 27th June 1975 where the President enforced the powers conferred by Article 359(1) of the Constitution. In exercise of these powers, the right of any person including a foreigner to move to the court for the enforcement of Article 14, 21 and 22 of the Constitution and the proceedings pending in any court relating to the enforcement of the above-mentioned articles will be curtailed.

The main issue involved in this case was "Whether the High Court can entertain a writ of Habeas Corpus filed by a person where he challenges the ground for his detention, in the case where such person has been detained in the execution of the Presidential Orders.

In this case, four judges – Chief Justice A.N. Ray, along with Y.V. Chandrachud, Justices M.H. Beg and P.N. Bhagwati arrived at the conclusion, that is, while a proclamation of emergency is in operation under Article 359 (1), the writ of habeas corpus is not maintainable.

The four judges observed that no authority or powers lie with the courts to challenge the detention made under Sec 16A(9)b of the Maintenance of Internal Security Act (which provides that the person against whom a detention order is passed under Section 3 shall not be entitled to the communication or disclosure of any such ground, information or material as is referred to in clause (a) or the production to him of any document containing such ground, information or material) as it is clearly stated under the Act that the disclosure of grounds of detention need not be done.

Hence the court cannot challenge the order and can not question the state or the executive body to validate the detention. Hence no locus standi exists, so the party can not move to any court for maintaining suit on fundamental rights.

Justice Khanna gave a dissenting opinion and observed that while the proclamation of emergency is in operation, the person can not move to the court for enforcement of fundamental rights but that does not prevent him from exercising his legal remedy through the statute.

Justice Khanna exclusively relied on the judgment delivered in the case of Makhan Singh v. State of Punjab in which he specified: If a person while challenging the validity of his detention order, pleads any right which is outside the scope of rights mentioned in the order, his right to move to any court is not suspended, as it is outside the rights specified in the order as well as the Presidential order itself. Let's suppose a case where a person has violated the mandatory provisions of this Act, and due to this violation, he has been detained.

So, the detenu can contend that he has been illegally detained on the ground that the mandatory provisions of the Act have not been contravened. Such a plea is outside Article 359(1) and the right of the detenu to move for his release on such a ground cannot be affected by the Presidential order". Curtailment of Article 21 leads to deprivation of the right to life and personal liberty which is against the fundamental right ensured to every citizen of India since birth, along with the rights guaranteed by the Universal Declaration of Human Rights.

Duty of the Union to protect the States

It is the duty of the Union to ensure that the State remains protected from disturbance and external aggression, while the Proclamation of Emergency is in operation. The Union shall ensure that the State Government works according to the provisions of the Constitution.

State Emergency

As per Article 356, if the President after receiving a report from the Governor of a State or otherwise is satisfied that such a situation exists where the Government of a State cannot be carried in accordance with the provisions of the Constitution, he may issue a Proclamation.

Duration

When a Proclamation is issued under Article 356, it shall be first laid before each House of the Parliament. Such Proclamation shall remain in operation for 2 months unless before the expiry of the said period it has been approved by both Houses of the Parliament according to Article 356(3). Suppose in a case where the Lok Sabha has been dissolved during the issuance of a proclamation of emergency or its dissolution takes place within the above said period of two months and the Rajya Sabha has approved the Proclamation but the Lok Sabha has not approved it.

In such a case, the said proclamation shall not operate unless before the expiry of 30 days it has also been passed by the Lok Sabha after its reconstruction. The Proclamation will remain in operation for 6 months after it has been approved by the Parliament. The duration of an emergency can be extended for 6 months at a time but it cannot remain in operation for more than 3 years.

Revocation

By a subsequent Proclamation, a proclamation of State Emergency can be revoked.

Effects

State Emergency shall have the following effects:

1. The President shall have all the powers that are exercisable by the Governor in the State.

2. The President shall declare that the State shall exercise its Legislative powers by or under the authority of the Parliament.

3. If the President deems fit that necessary provisions shall be made to serve the purpose of the Proclamation, then he may make such provisions.

Difference between Articles 352 and 356

- Under Article 352, the State Legislature and Executive continue to function but the Centre gets the concurrent powers of the legislation and administration in the matters of the State. Under Article 356, the executive, as well as legislative power, is vested in the Centre and the State Legislature is dissolved.

- Under Article 352, the relationship between the Centre and all the States changes but in the case of Article 356 the relationship between the Centre and the State in which President's Rule is applied undergo a change.

Financial Emergency

As per Article 360, a Proclamation of Financial Emergency may be issued, if the President is of the opinion that such a situation exists where the financial stability of India or any part of the territory is threatened.

Duration

The Proclamation of Financial Emergency shall cease to operate after 2 months unless it has been approved by both the Houses of Parliament. In a case where during the issuance of Proclamation the Lok Sabha has been dissolved or its dissolution takes place within the said period of 2 months and the Rajya Sabha has approved the proclamation but the Lok Sabha has not approved it. Then, such a proclamation shall not operate unless before the expiry of 30 days Lok Sabha has passed a resolution approving proclamation.

Revocation

By a subsequent Proclamation, Proclamation of Financial Emergency can be revoked.

Effects

Financial Emergency has the following effects:

- The executive authority of the Union shall give directions to the State regarding the maintenance of financial stability.

- It may include provisions for reduction of salaries and allowances of all or any class of persons serving in the State. This includes Judges of the High Court and the Supreme Court.
- The Money Bills shall be reserved for the approval of the President.

Conclusion

Having dealt with all emergency provisions, it is easy to understand the purpose behind the enforcement of such provisions. But it is important to note that even when these provisions are provided for the nation's security and protection of the people, the provisions in themselves give drastic discretionary powers in the hands of the Executive. This affects the federal structure of the nation and essentially turns it into a unitary one.

Therefore, the courts should be given the power to expand the powers of the Centre, as the same will act as a built-in mechanism to check if the discretionary powers are being used arbitrarily by the Parliament and the Executive.